# WHAT GOES DOWN

## The End of an Eating Disorder

*By Callie Bowld*

**What Goes Down**

First published in 2018 via CreateSpace and Kindle Direct Publishing.

# TABLE OF CONTENTS

To all of the Callies out there:

You are not alone.  You are not weak.
You are brass and bold and stronger than this disease.
You are.

Let this be your story, your victory, your new beginning, too.

# PROLOGUE

## A WORD ON HUMOR: WALLS INTO WINDOWS

*A great piece of comedy is a verbal magic trick, where you think it's going over here—and then all of a sudden you're transported over here. And there's this mental delight that's followed by the physical response of laughter, which, not coincidentally, releases endorphins in the brain.*

*And just like that, you've been seduced into a different way of looking at something because the endorphins have brought down your defenses. This is the exact opposite of the way that anger and fear and panic, all of the flight-or-fight responses, operate.*

*Flight-or-fight releases adrenalin, which throws our walls up sky-high. And then comedy comes along, dealing with a lot of the same areas where our defenses are the strongest—race, religion, politics, sexuality—only by approaching them through humor instead of adrenalin, we get endorphins and the alchemy of laughter turns our walls into windows, revealing a fresh and unexpected point of view.*

**Chris Bliss, Comedian**

Humor. It is the most difficult way to approach a sensitive subject because it seems to make light of it, it flirts on the verge of offensive. But, if done expertly, it can be the most effective tool because it sneaks up quietly and slips into your conscience while your guard is down. *"It's just comedy. Nothing serious about it."* Then all of a sudden you've seen something big and important in a very different light, and it is now all too serious. But it is also now true and undeniable, because you laughed at it. This is what humor can do. It can allow me to help you *see* the blunt reality of your life with an eating disorder and finally decide to stop damaging yourself. By the time you've laughed, you can't take it back or un-see the honest truth exposed and I hope it will give you the strength you've been looking for to change it. Walls into windows.

*Comedy is filled with surprise, so when I cross a line, I like to find out where the line might be and then cross it deliberately, and then make the audience happy about crossing the line with me.*

### George Carlin, Comedian

I feel like I'm sashaying saucily up to you: "Would you like me to seduce you?" Let's see if I can.

I distinctly recall the first time I tried to make myself throw up. Poised tentatively in front of the bowl, staring into the water, not sure if I was really about to do what I was thinking about doing. *"Really Callie?"* Then I did it. I jammed an awkward hand in, not knowing why or what I was doing but shoving it back there anyway—like a horny teenage boy trying to lose his virginity to a belly button—because something *had to* work. What I just did, all that naughty food I just ate, *had to be* undone. And you may imagine me as a sad teen, a hurt high school student. I was not. I was nearing thirty. About to get my J.D. And, I remember thinking for a fleeting second, as my dry throat was revolting in pain, what, exactly, in my life needed such extreme *fixing*? What had brought me to my knees on a grimy floor in front of a toilet? What was so terribly wrong that I … ? Then before my mind could answer, my body responded. Foul chunks ripped through my throat and it was done. A little lever in my mind was flipped.

*click*

I then knew I could do it. I had a whole new weapon in my eating disorder arsenal. Years before, I had chosen to make food my enemy. I had committed to punishing my body until it turned skinny and pretty, which meant nothing hurtful or bad would ever happen to me again. To accomplish that, I vowed to extract whatever way possible, whatever calories I had just put in because I told myself every single one was bad for me. Every single one that went in, they all had to come out. The 'how' did not matter, simply the 'out.' And now, I had found a new, way-easier-than-working-out *way*, to accomplish my all-necessary 'out.' The yang to my 'in.' Honestly, the first time I threw up, I felt happy. Relieved that food was out of me. I had found an answer. A solution. *"I'm in control, people! Can't you see?"*

My hand was covered in blood and gut slime, the taste and smell of it almost making me heave solely out of repulsion as I pushed it back into my mouth, sliding across my lips. But I kept at it. I didn't know then that the trick was to not let it touch anything until it was past my taste buds. You see? I know tricks. About how to be a good bulimic. So, really none of us need to *stop*; we just need to get *better* at it. I should become an instructor! Imagine me—in a floor-length black gown, tight bun and whip in hand (I believe this would be the appropriate attire, and who doesn't like yielding a whip?)—standing before a room full of skinny girls, all curled over their own toilet which now takes the place of their desk. "Tssk, tssk ladies! Two fingers, not three!" *whap!*

And there went the line. We just crossed it. Humor, you saucy little vixen you! But maybe you didn't. Maybe you're still standing stubbornly on the other side, your foul hands crossed over your bony chest, your red sweaty, snot-strewn face shaking 'no.' *"I like my little potty routine, thank you."* Maybe you don't want to be converted because maybe you feel the way I used to about my disorder: that it was the only available answer for me. *"Everyone else in the world can eat normal and look normal and have beautiful bodies, but not me. That doesn't work for me. I've tried it. I ate a bagel once and got so fat. For me, this is my only solution."*

Well, is it working?

We all know what I had just discovered—the fact that I could make myself throw up—was in no way the solution. Instead, I had just created the worst problem of my life. I had just planted the seed for a deeply-rooted, debilitating ten-year addiction.

You don't want a potty desk in my classroom because its laughable. It feels stupid and embarrassing, because it is. Incredibly dangerous too.

I share these vile moments to remind you, and myself, how repulsive it was. How repulsive *I* was. And how horribly I was treating this beautiful, strong, capable body of mine. Now that I have grown older and met people with despairingly sad health conditions—people who cannot easily walk a flight of stairs, who cannot swim, who cannot taste food, who have to empty the shit from their colostomy bag every couple of hours, people who cannot walk, run, surf, sing, climb—and I see that my body is thankfully, miraculously, by a stroke of sheer damn luck still able to do all of that and more. Yet some of the things I chose to do to it involved voluntary stomach convulsions, dry-heaving, sweating in the fetal position while an overdose of laxatives made their way through my miles of intestines, pressing a worried hand on my chest because my heart was beating so violently after a binge that I hoped pressure from the outside could somehow slow it down.

*Body, I'm sorry. So unbelievably sorry.*

Harboring an eating disorder is exceedingly selfish and completely indefensible when you imagine all of the people that would give anything to have the body you have, just as it is, or even with whatever extra pounds you deathly fear would instantly cake on if you (don't say it!) ate like a normal person. Those people would give anything to have your body and treat it right. The time I spent thinking about food, worrying about food, avoiding food, *eating* bad food, throwing up food, I could have done and experienced so many amazing things, including enjoying good food, which I now do every day. And it didn't turn me instantly into a fat heifer. It's a Christmas Miracle! And that's not even broaching the subject of the money I spent on my stupid food. Around forty dollars a day in my drive-thru days. We'll get there, that was my heyday. I should have won the Golden Toilet Award, with golden arches on top!

So, laughter. Humor. Comedy. It is intended not to belittle the danger and disgust of an eating disorder, but the *need* for it. Because there really is none. The hilarious truth of it all is that food is not the enemy, your messed-up mind is. The mere mention or thought of food triggers your mental response to immediately reject it, or plan how to eject it, without any real need to do either, but your mind refuses to let you believe that. It's like that snake eating its own tail. A fitting symbol for bulimia, right? Because if you follow it the other way, he's continuously throwing himself up, no? But once you stop the in-and-out, the down-then-back-up, you'll be amazed at how fantastic your overtly-grateful body will look and feel.

Why did this happen to me? Why did, as a hurt and scared teenager so many years ago, I flip that switch in my brain and cause myself to suffer an unnecessary disorder for so many years when I am a smart, capable, healthy woman? I don't have an exact answer for that. Because I'm very stubborn, driven, and exceedingly hard on myself. And I get royally pissed off when something hurts me and I respond irrationally. I decide to bend my poor body to my iron will and punish it for letting bad things happen to me? I don't quite know. All I know is I did it. For years and years. And hid it. For years and years. Maybe it was so I could become a voice for you and others, so I could save others from the same long-term horrid outcome. If that's one potential outcome, I know I will be proud. If this book saves one solitary person, it's worth every minute I put into it. I also know I have forgiven myself. And that it's okay to laugh at your mistakes, even the dangerous dumb ones. When you look back through all of your chapters—all the ironic coincidences and the trails and turns you took, and the times you found it all circled back anyway despite your best efforts—you have to find that life is just ... funny. I certainly think so.

So, let's get you healed already. If I was there with you, I would hold this book up and slam it against your forehead: "The power of my charisma compels you!" *bam!*

Now, go make some popcorn to nibble on slowly—so you'll stop thinking about all the other fatty, greasy, cheesy things you want to eat right now because you're sitting still, you're hungry and it's gnawing at you—and stay focused. Keep reading. Normalcy, happiness, and a healthier you awaits.

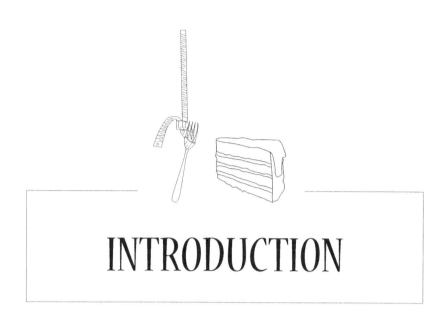

# INTRODUCTION

**WHAT GOES DOWN: IN A DISORDERLY MIND**

Whether you are a full-blown bulimic, a habitual binge-eater, or just a chronic yo-yo dieter who is just starting to slip down the slope toward an eating disorder, this is where you are headed. This is how difficult, disgusting, and exhausting your life is about to become. This was the torturous mental tape I played daily. Over and over. For years.

"Let's just pop in here and get a burger," your friend says to you, which immediately makes her no longer your friend. "I'm starving," she says. And you are too. But you're *always* starving. You've spent half of your adult life feeling hungry. Fighting hungry. Shushing hungry.

But, you have an eating disorder. You can't just eat ... A burger. What goes down—in a disorderly mind?

*A burger, are you insane?*
*Do you know how many grams of fat are in there?*
*How many grams of fat are in there?*
*Those go right to my thighs. Yep, thigh calories.*
*And burgers come on a bun. Bread?! Please!*
*And burgers always come with fries. Fuck!*
*Why can't they have those cool lettuce-wrapped burgers that Burger King did for a while?*
*Shit, they're not going to have anything other than burgers.*
*And fries. Grease sticks ... really?*
*And, we're going somewhere after this. I can't ...*
*Maybe it's a single stall and there's a lock on the door ...*
*How long will that stay in my stomach? Maybe I can do it later?*
*Maybe I can just have a few bites.*
*And some fries. Mostly with ketchup.*
*Ketchup's a vegetable, right?*
*Damn burgers! Damn friend!*
*Damn ME! Why does this have to be so hard?*

It doesn't. But you don't know that. You can't see that. Rather, this torturous inner dialogue all plays out in about the span of three seconds before you sheepishly say, "Okay." If it's a good friend who knows you really well and knows you struggle with food (likely not; most people in your life have no clue), he or she will see the twist on your face in those three seconds and call you out on your shit: "It's. Just. A. Burger." But they love you and care about you and know, for whatever reason, for you, it's just tough. For you, food just ignites some weird internal struggle and gets you all anxious and balled-up inside. So she'll add: "We'll share. And you don't have to have any fries." *That's a good friend, right there. Keep her.*

But this will happen often when you get caught in what I used to call a "food jam." A forced meal. A real dilemma. For me, lunch was always the most common. When I was a highly-functional bulimic I would often starve through the day, drinking only coffee for breakfast. *"Why blow through so many calories so early? When I'm not even desperately starving yet?"* I would then—if I didn't get caught in a food jam at lunch—have a little nibble around noon, preferably a light salad or a little Special K bar (because those eighty calories are really going to hold you up). That would leave me with a whole saved-up bank of "food points" (those were real in my world) to spend that evening. Because the evening was when I liked to spend them, according to my pre-set, private, everyday routine. But, if someone wanted to go out for lunch, sometimes this would blow my whole plan. *A damn food jam!*

When I did join the normal folks, for a normal meal out, I was known to *always* order the salad when eating out, nothing else, while my normal friends and colleagues would order and eat normal things like sandwiches, soups, burgers, whatever. Sometimes (because I was starving) I would start nibbling on the crackers that came with my salad. Then perhaps one of the biscuits or cornbread they brought to the table. Then another; because, remember, I'm starving. Then perhaps a bite of a friend's burger. "Just a bite," I'd say with a smile. But as I swallowed that glorious burger bite I knew I was done. I'd crossed that "two-bites-too-many" line and suddenly everything had to come up. I had to drop everything for an hour during the middle of my busy lawyer day to fill the tank and pump it out. I had to. Because my stupid friend wanted to go out for lunch and my stupid body ate a bite of a burger. And, now you see why it's called a food jam. You can probably also see why I didn't have many lunch dates. *"Eat, rather than work, through lunch? Who has time for that?"* I usually didn't.

So, let's assume on a pretty average day, I'm able to do my lettuce-and-vinegar or Special K lunch routine, leaving my imaginary 1,500 food points to gloriously spend that evening. In real numbers, we're probably talking about the additional 1,500 calories I still *needed* to put in just to barely feed my body for the day. But do note, I already chose to do it in an irrational "back-loading" way where my choice is to basically starve all day, preparing to binge all night; so even if I take in an acceptable number of calories by day's end, I haven't spaced them out in any kind of healthy way to keep my metabolism up or my body properly fueled. So, I've already screwed myself over. But, let's forget all that and just see it for what it is: 1,500 food points I have now to spend. *"Whoopee!"*

I then had two options. I could (a) binge and purge that evening, preferably once, sometimes multiple times, to the point of exhaustion, so that I could fall quickly asleep before the urge to eat sucked me down again. Sadly, this was often a way I looked forward to spending the evening. Passing fatty, cheesy, greasy foods past my lips while curled up on the couch, watching mindless TV. Then five minutes undoing it. *Never happened.* With the option to start right back in again if I wanted to, my half-eaten smorgasbord of food awaiting me on the coffee table. To me, that was a blissful way to spend the evening. Indulging myself with no one around to judge me.

Obviously I lived alone.

Or I could (b) justifiably gorge on a healthy dinner, even eating and keeping down what my disorderly-mind considered semi-bad foods. *Microwave veggies in a light butter sauce? Ummmm*

*... okay. But just three boxes, not four.* And, because I'd starved all day and kept down a meal that wasn't guaranteed to turn to insta-cheese on my thighs, I could wake the next day, even after four microwave-box-whatevers, and not feel like a total cow. But, what goes down ... must come back up ... or it must be worked off. This is the classic sign of an eating disorder. In and out. Everything is accounted for.

So if I, trying to be strong, chose option (b) and decided to actually eat something, like normal people do, by putting mouthfuls in, swallowing them and keeping them down. LIKE NORMAL PEOPLE DO! Then, I had to at least work those nasty food calories off. I couldn't just let food go in and sit there. *"Are you crazy?"* Jesus, the strenuous, exhausting workouts I used to make myself do, over a box of damn veggies. I would usually workout right before dinner because dinner was the ultimate reward. The Food Point Casino! I could jog for miles thinking about what delicious savory rewards awaited. *"A cracker ... No three!"* I would dream, as my feet pounded the pavement. And, because I was starved for calories—my body begging and pleading for fuel—I would often get light-headed. See stars. Pee my pants. I'm not kidding. My head would spin. My ears would pop. Very strange things happened. The little guy in my head was running around, flipping all sorts of switches and buzzers trying to get me to stop and do what normal people do. Just eat normal. Workout normal. And treat my beautiful, strong body right.

*"Shut up little man. That's what weak people do and I'm stronger than them."*

Stupider, too. I hate to say it, but I was sometimes proud when, after a workout, I would have strange sensations like this. Signs to a normal person that I had pushed myself too hard were signs to me that I was a full-blooded thoroughbred. *Way to go self!*

I was such an idiot. A foolish, dangerous idiot. But stubborn, too. Even after I had wrenched my body horrifically over the toilet until I was sure every last fat-laden calorie had come back out, if I burped later and tasted cheeseburger, panic would set in. There must still be some left inside.

*"Time to go jog till I see stars."* And off I went. This would happen over and over again. It was my continuous loop. I wonder sometimes how I was even able to study, work, write, and accomplish all of the very impressive things I did during that time—college, law school, passing the Bar Exam, becoming a trial lawyer—all while I kept this ridiculous, exhausting in-and-out routine. I truly think it takes a Type A person to maintain an eating disorder. Through some sick re-wiring of our brains, we take pride in how much punishment we can inflict on ourselves. Have you ever felt that way? Well, here's the thing. Do you know who cares that you can exercise until you faint, make yourself hurl until your stomach is concave?

NO ONE.

Absolutely no one. The number of people you are impressing? ZERO. In fact, if most people saw the rigorous lengths you go to, only to fail time and time again at what you are trying to accomplish (to look and feel good), they would in no way be impressed. They would be horrified, sad, and embarrassed for you. They would think, if you can't see the ridiculousness of what you're doing to yourself, then you must be a pathetic joke. The armless Sisyphus with cracked, bleeding teeth.

That's harsh, I know. But it's exactly why you work so hard to hide it. You know the shame you would feel if anyone found out, because it is gross. It is embarrassing. It is weird. And you have to come to terms with that. You hide it because if anyone knew—if anyone could watch you stuffing your fat face, shuffling toward the toilet with your pants unbuttoned and your body hunched over (because your belly is so distended you literally cannot stand up straight), and shoving your repulsive vomit-covered hand into your mouth time and time again—they would feel embarrassed for you. They would probably no longer want to spend time with you, work with you, shake your hand, or think about this: kiss you, touch you, have sex with you.

I hope some of this is really hitting home for you. Is whatever release, pleasure, or mental empowerment you feel you get from starving or binging worth losing all of that: friends, your job, your lover? Even perhaps your life? Just because you wanted so badly the rush of pleasure you get from eating a whole cake? Where might that rush lead you?

*Eating disorders have the highest mortality rate of any mental illness.*
http://www.anad.org/get-information/about-eating-disorders/eating-disorders-statistics/

What you are doing shows only that you are weak. Nothing more. A stronger person can eat just one piece of cake and have their life, too.

Be that person.

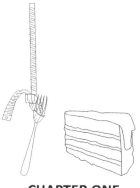

**CHAPTER ONE**

# HOW IT STARTS: A CARE BEAR TUMMY

How did all of this begin for me? What was the root? For some, that may be a difficult question to answer. For me, it's not. While the watering of the seed, the growth of the disease, and my decision to actually start nurturing a disorder was a far more difficult question for me to answer, pinpointing the seed was not. For me, this all started with my rotund muscular gut that pooches out further than my tits. I have a Care Bear tummy.

But, everyone has one—not an eating disorder, thank God—but a part of their body they hate. Anyone with an eating disorder likely has three. Most people, healthy or otherwise, have some part of their body that they hate. But for someone with an eating disorder, we do not just *hate* this part. We *loathe* and *despise* it. We may often pinch, punch, or scream at it. If we could take a scalpel and cut it off our bodies, we would. No matter how much it might hurt or how much it might cost. There's a reason they call plastic surgery *cosmetic.* It's all about looking good; changing some part about yourself that you have decided is so hideous, so unacceptable, that you literally can no longer live with it. It must be surgically changed.

It may be tiny, wayward tits. Chunky blubberous fat around your tummy that jiggles hideously when you jog in place in front of the mirror (*because we all do that*). Pounds of cottage cheese on your thighs. Big, bulbous upper arms that have forbidden you from ever wearing anything short-sleeved. Whatever yours is, this is the part of your body that you will always instantly shield once it is exposed, that is if you ever let it be exposed. It's the area you pull and stretch clothing around every time you sit down or stand up. When you sit, you double over and cover it as best you can with your hands and arms. *"Oh God, don't look there. Look anywhere but* there*!"* The thought of going to the beach, where people wear bathing suits, makes you nauseous because you know *it* will have to come, too: that stupid, despised part.

For me, as it is for many women and men who struggle with their weight, it was my stomach. My big, muscular, rotund stomach. While I am of normal height and build, my stocky gymnast body does have one very unfortunate downside. My ribs and hips are literally about six inches apart. I have a short, squashed boxy frame. With no beautiful curvy hips to stretch and thin out my stomach, it tends to protrude in one direction and one direction only. *"Onward and outward!"* shouts my tummy, leading the pack. I can literally push my tummy out and look like I'm six months pregnant. I'm not kidding. I am a trophy-carrying Biggest Pooch award winner. It's really a little frightening to watch. I've never measured it before, but I believe it protrudes about eight inches out from its normal position. Six to eight at least. It does this both when I push it out intentionally and when I forget to suck in. I can go from looking like a somewhat healthy, fit person to a total fatty by simply forgetting to suck in, which for normal people is about 98.2% of their day. Don't ask me how often I suck in. Not yet anyway. We'll get there.

And each time I think about my Care Bear tummy, I see it as I did when my hatred of it first began: bulging out above my hand-covered crotch, stealing the show, even, from my exposed man-shaped tits and the lampshade covering my head. Ahh … my lampshade moment. We'll get there, too. Just wait. Good times lie ahead.

But, what do I always fail to mention, acknowledge or even remotely appreciate when I am bashing my despised part, my stupid, horrible three-rolled tummy? Its incredible strength. I have a super-solid, sporty core. I was a gymnast for years. I tumbled and cheered, launched and caught many of my fair share of stick-thin cheer blondes. I also played rugby some in college, and club soccer. Now, an adult in my mid-thirties, I am still capable of aerialist feats, adventure sports (kite-surfing, skiing, offshore sailing, and aerial silks). With all of the many thousands of pounds I have lifted and carried over the years, I have never once had a back problem. Why? Because I have a stodgy, pooches-out-when-I-sit core. Now when I meet people my same age or not much older who—because of obesity, illness, injury, etc.—cannot walk up a flight of stairs, pick up anything over twenty pounds, much less surf, ski, hike, climb, dive, or swim, I am reminded how incredibly grateful I am to be healthy! Just healthy. I honestly can't think of anything that my amazing body, which includes my muscular protruding gut, would prevent me from trying.

Honestly try to imagine yourself laying in a hospital bed—perhaps after a car accident that has shattered your pelvis and legs, or with a progressive cancer that's not likely to go away—and you would give *anything* to have the <u>exact body you have now</u> and would be damn proud of it. Let those tiny, wayward tits fly while you paraglide, mountain-climb, and surf. Who gives a crap if your thighs are jiggling as you run a marathon, play tag football with your kids, join a beach volleyball team, or go scuba-diving. All of the beautiful, captivating little fish down there who will mesmerize you don't give a flying flip that your thighs are a little cheesy. So why should you? Enough at least to hide them, loathe them, or do terrible things to your body in the sole effort to excise them. Terribly unproductive things, too, I might add. Things that will never make that part of your body look the way you want it too. Because here's the thing:

It's likely no amount of extreme dieting, starvation, intense exercising, even horrific binging and purging, and perhaps cosmetic surgery is ever going to change that part that you hate. Because that part is never going to change. Did you hear me?

Never. Not ever. Because it can't.

Not entirely anyway. Not to the point you are imagining it. It's likely whatever vision you're implanting in your mind—the way *you* want so desperately to look—is not and can never be you; because of genetics, physical make-up, muscular build, a thousand things that make you YOU. The only one in the world. You. The only person that can be you. There's probably thousands of people in far worse physical condition than you, dozens of pounds heavier, who are similarly starving and punishing themselves trying to get down to some smaller, skinnier, not-so-fat size. Imagine if the image in their mind is you. They're trying to become you. And, why will they never be able to achieve that?

Because there is only one YOU.

Why can't you look like Cindy Crawford? Because there is only one Cindy Crawford. And that ain't you my friend! (*Unless, Cindy, my Eternal Goddess, if you're reading this, we love (and kind of hate) you!*) But that's totally okay, because do you know who Cindy Crawford is not and can never be?

Are you feeling me now?

It took me a long time to realize this, but I finally did. No matter how much I dieted, how little food I put in, or what astounding quantities I ejected out, it did not magically morph my muscular boxy gut into a beautiful lingerie model's demure, long tummy. It did not magically change into a sleek, sexy Crawford tummy. *"What?! Why not! That's not fair."* You. Stupid you. Dieting will never change a part of your body that's genetic. It will not make your tits un-wayward. If you have a pear-shaped body with meaty thighs, they're probably always going to be meaty and a little cheesy no matter how much weight you lose, no matter how flat your tummy becomes. In fact, for me, the terrible dieting and eating habits made my stomach look *worse*. My trying-to-survive tummy would store the fat my body knew it was going to need later (because I was a horrible body owner and I repeatedly starved it), which would make it protrude even more. Also, it often came tumbling out because my body, starved of energy, was too tired to stand up straight and hold it in to maintain good posture and because it was so stretched out from over-eating.

Are you hearing me? Everything unhealthy I did to try and "fix" my tummy did the exact opposite.

Even in my very early eating disorder days—when I dropped thirty pounds, my backbone poking through as little nobs on my neck, my hip bones jutting out like that of a dying cow—I still hated my tummy. Maybe more than ever because it could still double over and look "fat" even when I was anything but. It still pooched out when I forgot to suck in, probably even more so because my other body parts were so want and concave, because my belly (the bulk of my meat and core strength) was trying to stay strong for everyone else. She was trying her best to hold us all together.

I say all of this because what took me years to realize is that, for many, whatever your "despised part" is (tits, ass, tummy, cankles, caveman arms, whatever) dieting, no matter how extreme, will not change it. Rather, doing unhealthy things to your body because of it will likely only warp your perception of it or, in reality, make that part look worse and more pronounced. What I have found about my stocky Care Bear tummy is that it looks its best when the other parts around it are healthy and filled out. That is when my big muscular stomach is the least noticeable.

The first weight I lost when I began withholding food was my boobs. They shriveled. *"Thanks boobs."* But push-up bras can fix that so I didn't really care. It's not like most of us are really striving to look good *naked*. (Once someone's got your knickers off, they're not likely going to turn and run just because you have a muffin top, am I right?) No, we're trying to look good in *clothes*. When we go out in *public*. When people's eyes are on us. That's when we want to look thin and beautiful. That's why tummies, asses, and thighs are typically the most dreaded part. They can't be hidden or manipulated quite as easily as boobs. Before Spanx, that was. That is some good sci-fi wonder-stretch shit there. *Thank you, Oprah!*

But let's go back in time, to when I do not know all of this. To when my Care Bear tummy is the root of all the problems in my life. To a time when I think I have all the answers. I think I'm in control. I think I can fix my body by torturing it. And I start here, with my stomach, because while many eating disorders start with a vicious, mean mother, pageants, modeling, athletes that need to stay thin to perform, or school bullies that call you "fat," I also think for many others that's not how it starts at all. You may not have been fat enough to be taunted in school. You may have had a perfectly normal-sized body and you may have had a supporting, loving family that loved the way you looked and told you so. Yet, you developed this sickness anyway. Maybe you're just a normal person that didn't have any of the most talked-about triggers or causes of an eating disorder, you just have that part. The part of your body that you hate. That you are desperate to change.

It can start as simply as there.

Looking back, I am so lucky my strong, amazing tummy stuck with me long enough to see me through all of the horrendous punishment I put her through and came out stronger and healthier on the other side. That's not how it ends up for many people who ravage their body with eating disorders. It can end with heart failure, persistent electrolyte imbalance, irritable bowel syndrome, a colostomy bag (do you even want to imagine the rest of your life with that?), permanent ulcers, pancreatitis, osteoporosis, loss of hair and skin elasticity (I experienced that), rotted yellow teeth, and yellow fingers (check, check), not to mention horrific gastric rupture or tearing of your throat, assuming it doesn't end in death.

Because it can end there. I'm not exaggerating. I don't do that.

*Every 62 minutes at least one person dies as a direct result from an eating disorder.*
http://www.anad.org/get-information/about-eating-disorders/
eating-disorders-statistics/

Your life is worth so much more than whatever body part you are so furiously fighting.

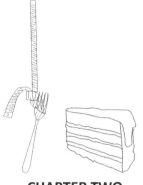

# CHAPTER TWO

# HOW IT TAKES ROOT: CONFIDENCE CRUMBLING, MIND BLAMES BODY

So how does an eating disorder actually develop? How does one go from not just despising a certain part (or parts) of their body, but becoming so irreconcilably disappointed with their body that they decide to take action, to deprive it, to punish it? (While, mind you, taking into <u>no</u> account how good their body feels and functions, because *that's* not important. Not at all.)

For me, it started with a Polaroid. A lampshade. A stocky topless girl. And a Polaroid. Then, later, a traumatic Tanya Harding whack to the knees of my confidence that briefly shattered me. That was just the pinnacle moment that triggered what had already been brewing in my mind and what would continue to roar like a furnace long after I could even recall what Tanya's club felt like. Many things had been leading up to it.

My body is, by nature, stocky, boxy, and muscular. In middle and high school, I was a gymnast. Gymnast first. Cheerleader second, but I definitely had, and will always have, the thick, toned body of a gymnast. I'm sure many of you are thinking *"Well, damn, I can't listen to her because she already has the perfect body. I'd kill for a thick, gymnast body."* Trust me, whatever your body looks like, there are probably many who would give anything to spend just one day in it. We all do it to ourselves—grass is greener, she is skinnier, he is happier. It's just a syndrome. No matter how beautiful our bodies are, we (inside our minds) see only the flaws. Particularly that despised part. My hatred of my rotund, muscular gut began long before college.

I didn't start my period until I was sixteen. And, I didn't even start it like normal women; it had to be medically-induced. Because I was highly athletic, as is the same with many gymnasts, my puberty was delayed. At fifteen (when all the other girls, it seemed, had started years ago and were all wearing bras), I begged and pleaded with my mom to put me on birth control (not to have sex—no, no!—I was way too hideous of a chunk for any guy to want me then). But I had heard birth control could kick-start your puberty. To be honest, it's not that I wanted my period. That shit's gross. I was just sick of being embarrassed by the girls in gym who made fun of me because I didn't have any hair. You know … down *there*. (Which, looking back, as long as the boobs had come in, I wouldn't have minded a perfectly smooth no-maintenance little lady down there. Wouldn't that be nice?) But at the time I was horribly flat-chested. Except that I wasn't like an ironing board. No, that would require a flat stomach, remember? What do I have? The hideous monster gut. My "skeeter bites" were like two little road signs marking the path up to Mount Care Bear. Anytime I didn't remember to suck my stomach entirely in (which is, what, about 95% of everyone's day?), my gut would stick out like I was six months pregnant.

I'm not kidding. I have an incredibly short midsection. The distance from my ribs to my pelvis (when I straighten up) is probably less than six inches. And it's packed with muscle. If I let the avalanche go, she usually hits so hard against the table, it pushes my chair back.

My God I hated my stomach. But, Jesus, what I have learned now about posture, posing, slouching, could have saved me years of food anxiety and eating stress. By the time I turned sixteen, I had thankfully met a guy kind enough to show some interest in me and we'd been pawing around at each other, often causing more pain than pleasure, and now we were ready to do it! First Boyfriend and I were ready to cut the ribbon. At least then I finally had some real cards to play with my mom. While I was sixteen and still hadn't started my period (which, believe it or not, qualifies as morbidly-embarrassing for a sixteen-year-old girl), now the boyfriend and I were ready to have sex. *"Take that, Mom!"* That turned out to be reason enough and she finally got me on the pill. A regular flow finally started, and the boyfriend seemed to somehow find a way around my monster gut, enough, at least, for us to practice a little in the stationary position. Life was pretty good. Then there was this photo.

Did it start with a photo for you? One where perhaps you are slouched over, you've got some rolls bulging out, you're heavier than you would like to be and you feel like you are the grossest person on the planet? That no one in their right mind should ever want to touch you? How can just a photo do that?

But we all know it can.

Twice I decided to totally fuck my life up, because of a single photo. One particular position my body was in at one particular moment. One snap in time emblazed itself on my brain as an unforgivably-unflattering status I had let my disobedient body attain because I didn't have a death grip on the controls. That image dictated my mindset for years after.

So, the first photo. It was on a choir trip. (And, just as an aside, if you thought the kinky shenanigans that go down at Band Camp were wild, you couldn't fathom what choir kids come up with when we travel.) A handful of other altos and I were hanging out in one of our hotel rooms, thinking we were a big deal sipping stolen vodka when one of the girls pulled out a Polaroid camera and fired up the stupid train:

"Let's take pictures!" said one.
"Ooh, naughty ones!" said another.
"Not too porney, though," because that was a word then.
"Let's put a lampshade on our heads!"
"Perfect!"
"Then show them to guys and see if they can tell who's who!"
"Perfect-er!"

I told you, we were brilliant. But it honestly did sound kind of silly and fun. What else were we doing? Practicing our hymnals? Pssshhh! We couldn't leave the room. We were already a little tipsy. So each of us started stripping and lining up for our first topless photo. Exciting milestone!

We all decided to put our hands over our crotches to cover them. To, you know, keep our topless lampshade photos classy. But you know what you look like when you let your shoulders slump inward and your hands drop down to your crotch. It's almost impossible to hold good posture while your arms are reaching down toward your genitals. At least it is for me. But honestly, I was so worried about whether my little Tinker Tits were looking good, I forgot for a moment all about my monstrous belly. And you might be thinking: *"Awesome! Great! You finally let that go!"* You. Silly you.

Because it was this photo that would prevent me from "letting that go" for years. I didn't even suck in. I just dropped my arms down, tried to think big titty thoughts and *snap* it was done. I was handed my token and I started waving it around in the air until the image took shape. Thankfully, the other girls were too enamored with their own photos and the lampshade process that was still going on to see my face when my body formed on the film.

I didn't even look like a girl. In my mind, anyway. My stomach was huge! And because my shoulders were slumped down with my arms pushing against my boobs, they didn't even look like boobs. Honestly, I looked like a chubby teenage boy. I'm not kidding. A boy.

"Callie, let us see!" Some of the girls started to peek over my shoulder. Silence fell.

"Are you going to show your boyfriend?" they asked.

I almost cried. Right then and there, a puddle of stupid *"I'm fat and ugly"* tears. But the revelation that my ugly, misshapen body was no longer just an image in my mind—it had now been proven by the hideous Polaroid in my hand to be an actual, real-life tangible object for others to see—caused me to knee-jerk react the same way I always do when something hurts me deeply. I made a joke about it. Tried to laugh it off. They didn't have to know it was real if I was kidding around about it.

"I don't think lampshades are going to be *my* new accessory," I said with a weak chuckle and walked over to the vodka bottle to take as big of a sip as I could handle, hoping the girls didn't read too much into it, that they didn't care enough about me to want to pry any deeper.

Thankfully, it turns out, they didn't. High school girls care primarily about very few things: how *they* look, how many boys like them, and how popular they are. So, focus was instantly diverted back to their photos and I pretended to look happily on while they giggled and pointed out things.

"I can tell you're laughing in this one, Stacey. Even though I can't see your face."
"I can tell this is Nikki. Look at those boobs!"
"I can tell ... " they continued on.

But only one thought kept pounding in my mind. *"I can tell they're all girls. Pretty, skinny girls."* My confidence was shattered. None of them had my monster gut. Even the ones with small boobs, the size of mine, had dainty shoulders and small rib cages so everything still looked in proportion. I was not being overly dramatic in realizing mine was easily the worst photo. I can tell you no one asked to see mine again. And no one asked if I was going to show it to my boyfriend again. *Not if I wanted to keep him,* they probably thought. And I agreed.

I couldn't wait to get away from the girls long enough to destroy that photo. But, then when I finally did find myself alone with it, later in the hotel bathroom, I found I wanted to keep it. To remind myself how hideous I was. To make sure I remembered to always suck in, always hold my shoulders back, always do anything to never look like that again. I believe that's when the thought first formed in my mind that my body needed punishing.

My crumbled confidence wasn't tied solely to how I looked, either. It wasn't just because all of the other girls looked more feminine than me. It was more vague than that. I felt like, if I was so different from them in that way, I must be different in so many other ways. I must not fit in with these people. They are somehow happier, blissfully less aware, yet somehow better than me. That is a feeling that, because it is not grounded exclusively in the one shallow sector of how I *look*, but rather in the multi-layered complex grid of who I *am*—different, not like them, disconnected—it took such an instant stronghold. It is also the reason my eating disorder was able to grow and get stronger no matter how many different sizes and shapes I morphed through during the twenty years that it was in control. Because my body seemed to be the cause of this massive degradation of my confidence, it became the target of my inner anger, and my mind seemed to disconnect from it in that moment. One being in charge of the other.

Is any of that striking a chord with you?

Once that happens, you don't see your body as an important part of you. It is no longer something that needs to be treated right, respected, fed nutritious fuel, and maintained with appropriate, healthy amounts of activity so that you—*the collective sum of your mind and body, YOU*—can look and feel good. No, it is the enemy. You hate your body. It's to be blamed for everything. It is the cause of everything bad in your life. And the only way to fix it—to make sure you don't have another one of those *"I'm so ugly and misshapen, I am different"* moments—is to pummel your body into something else. You believe you can turn it into a different body, one that will not cause you any embarrassment or pain. And, you are not thinking in any way of bone structure, metabolism, genetics, muscular build, any of that. The key to regaining control of your life becomes your control over food. What goes in and what comes out.

So, when you have that photo moment, that shock of how horrible and disgusting you look, your first instinct is to stop putting things in. *"I will stop eating as much and I will lose weight."* And it will work at first, but anorexia is hard. Hunger is so irritating. It gnaws at you, makes you feel antsy and frustrated. You have to try to keep your mind and hands busy at all times or they will drift toward food. It's hard to relax while intentionally depriving yourself of food. To maintain anorexia takes intense mental focus. It's exhausting, which means when you do finally decide to eat something, you are so hungry, so deprived that you go overboard. Just one bite too many brings on immense guilt in your mind for losing control. For letting your stupid body take over and try to feed itself. Then the all-consuming thought of how you're going to get that horrid food out of your body— even just the one excessive bite—takes over.

Exercise is often seen as the first possibility. *"I can't believe you ate the last bite of that sandwich. All that freaking bread?! I'll take care of this,"* your mind tells your body. Then you go run three miles because you, no wait your *body* ... ate the last bite of a sandwich. *"What a weakling she is!"* your mind screams to itself as your feet are pounding the pavement. Then, just like the focus and energy required to be anorexic began to exhaust you, so now does the ludicrous, completely-overboard exercise routine you've committed yourself to. You work out way too much, you feel faint and light-headed when you finish, and your body still has not become that other skinny, pretty, toned one it was supposed to; so you're still irritable, disappointed and now so, so tired. Hopeless and desperate for a solution to your every day, every hour "out" problem, you're open to any answer. Anything that can fix you. And all of this irritation, exhaustion, and anger at your body will bring you one day, weak and kneeling before a toilet, thinking about sticking your fingers down your own throat. I hope you can now see how it starts, grows, and progresses.

You will find yourself looking in the mirror constantly, lifting your shirt or lowering your pants to see if maybe—just maybe—you're starting to look better. Then when you see you aren't, you might start punching, slapping, and chastising your body. Starting to see it as an entirely different person, a being other than you, that is pathetic and weak. If you've ever found yourself looking at a photo, or in the mirror, or curled up in a ball of tears trying to push your disgusting flabby stomach in toward your backbone—treating your body as something removed from you—try to imagine this:

Imagine two people, both are exact replicas of you. But, one is in control. One, your mind, is carrying the whip. And Two, your body, is voiceless and unable to overtake the other. Imagine yourself slapping a plate of food away from Two's hands. Two looks up in utter confusion, scared, clueless, but submissive. "No food for you, Two! You fatty!" Then you shove Two out of her chair and onto the floor and begin to kick her towards a treadmill. "You were thinking about eating that food, Two. I know it. So run, you!" The treadmill starts and Two begins to jog, her eyes searching yours, pleading for an answer. An hour later, as Two is stumbling, falling over her own feet, about to faint from exhaustion, she watches in shock, as you stare at her with disgust and turn up the speed.

If that's not enough, imagine yourself forcing Two to kneel down before the bowl. You grip her hair at the base of her neck, pull hard and kick the back of her knees until she falls heavy onto them, her expression one of horror and confusion. Her eyes, wild with fear, lock on yours as you pull her mouth open and jam your hand in hard—all the way to the back of her throat then hold her head violently down over the toilet as she hurls. She comes up red-faced, the veins on her neck bulging, her mouth covered in slime, looking at you in full panic. Then you do it again. And again. And again. And there is nothing Two can do about it.

It is a horrifying show of disrespect and there is nothing your body can do to stop you from doing this to her. Other than to somehow fail. Let her throat rip open, her gut split and spew the foul contents out, her heart beat so hard and fast that it finally stops.

Unless you change your mind, abrupt failure that could kill or permanently disable or maim you, is the only way your body can finally get her only message through to you: *"Please stop. You're hurting me."*

This is where you're headed and it may all start with a photo; where you think you look fat and unlovable.

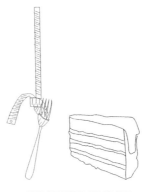

# CHAPTER THREE

# HOW IT TAKES OVER: CONFIDENCE CRUSHED, MIND TAKES CONTROL

I kept that first photo, the lampshade one, for several years. Looking at it on occasion, when for some reason I wanted to be reminded of how ugly I thought I really was. But, thankfully, I was also mostly happy and young, with a lot to distract me and a lot to look forward to. I was a cheerleader, a gymnast, I had a boyfriend and plans for college. And, more importantly, I was not living yet on my own, so I didn't have complete control over my diet. I wasn't exactly thrilled with the way my body looked, but I liked what it could do (flip, tumble, jump, lift, etc.). So the first whispers from my mind to do something about my body were too soft to truly influence me. Besides, I had a lot going on: prepping for the SAT and ACT, applying to colleges, while maintaining my grades and afterschool activities; not to mention falling in love with my boyfriend and spending so many hours professing my young teenage love for him. *"Ahhh ... sweet Boyfriend, let me count the ways."*

I was too busy to really think much about my eating habits, and didn't have the money or type of environment that would allow me to make very atypical choices about what I ate and how much. Cereal and milk were set on the table for breakfast, lunch was spent eating at the cafeteria with friends at school, and dinner was set before me in the evenings. I just ate normal, because there was really no other choice, and the image of that lampshade photo in my mind faded. I think, for many, it starts with a tiny seed. Packed lightly just beneath the soil—always there—but without water, sunshine, and nourishment, it just sits dormant. Then there is some culmination of stressors, changes in your life that find you stretched thin, overly stressed and worried, perhaps more pressure is put on you than ever before (perhaps you're the one putting that pressure on yourself, perhaps unnecessarily). Whatever the reason or cause, that alone may be enough: all of those stressors and worries continually mounting, until you start to slowly build a coping mechanism in your mind. And that mechanism may be food—a perverse deprivation of or over-indulgence in it.

I imagine the path is similar for many and different for others. For me, it was a seed I planted during puberty (well, my medically-induced hormonal jump-start that is, which I guess is in no way natural "puberty"). The seed was a realization that I have a body that is not slender and beautiful like other girls, which somehow makes me different and *less* than other girls. That seed was then nurtured by the stress of moving across country to live on my own for the first time, with no friends or acquaintances on campus, to begin college and start learning how to cope with all the demands of life as an independent adult. And as I was doing that, I found myself surrounded by throngs of gorgeous hourglass-shaped southern belles. This only continued the unraveling of my self-esteem, a pervasive waning of my confidence. Then the earth beneath my feet was blown upward in a scattering of dirt by a big, crushing bomb.

Once unearthed, my body laying weak and exposed on top of it, I imagine my seed then sprouting eight sinister roots that jutted upward and wrapped around my brain, my cerebrum, all the way down to my heart and stomach. The plant that emerged from the earth was black and sinewy, knotted, gnarly, and dense, bearing no fruit or leaves or anything of beauty, just thick black branches that filled my frontal lobe and gripped the backs of my eyeballs, making me see only my flaws and no one else's. For years this black growth would continue to tighten its hold on me, wrapping a new root and gnarly vine around a part of my insides each time I thought about quitting. Thought maybe my abusive approach to food was the real problem. Thought maybe all the torture I was forcing upon my body might be the reason it never looked the way I wanted it to. Thought maybe, just maybe, I should stop treating my body so horrifically and just see what might happen if I tried eating and exercising like a normal, healthy person. Each time one of those thoughts would creep in, like a tiny piece of fresh fruit growing in my mind, the wicked black bush inside that I had planted and nurtured would hunt it out, wrap its crackling vines around the lifeblood of the new plant, and squeeze until it turned black and shriveled, and eventually withered away.

For me, it started with a seed, then a heartbreaking bomb.

I had just graduated high school and moved across the country to start college at a top-rated state university. Good for me. I had worked very hard to get some scholarship money (which was extremely difficult as an out-of-state student) and had worked relentlessly back home as a waitress to save up enough to cover the remainder of my tuition, room and board. I was able to go to college. On my own, with no support, just my two feet, two hands, my incredibly stubborn brain, and an old beat-up car to get around. Fantastic for me. Most people would give anything for an opportunity like that, and I had it. I should have been happy and I shouldn't have given two shits whether I was ten pounds too heavy and indulged myself the occasional waffle or cupcake. I didn't. I started watering my "I hate my body" seed.

I had chosen an "Old South" school in Alabama where, unbeknownst to me, sororities are all that matters. You are nothing if you're not a legacy. The only reason you go to college is to look pretty, date a frat boy, have him "pin you" in a ridiculously-ceremonial ceremony, then get married, and have three beautiful blonde kids. Oh, all while being impossibly beautiful and skinny. And "Old South Skinny" was a new breed to me. Not only did these southern broads have exceptionally-slender waists—like circus-freaky, almost fits in two-cupped-hands waists—but they also had big, perfect, succulent boobs.

*"How the hell did they do that?"* Tantalizing curves *and* a torso so small you can't understand how their intestines fit? Maybe that's how they did it. Had their intestines removed and packed into their colossal tits. Smart bitches.

I felt like everyone was smarter than me, which is very stupid.

I had graduated high school with straight A's and had gotten a few small scholarships and grants to help cover some of the cost of my tuition at a highly-ranked state university. But I also felt very alone in my singular struggle. It seemed (although I know now this was a somewhat-accurate but also somewhat-skewed perception due to the ritzy, sorority gals I inadvertently surrounded myself with) that everyone else was going to college with help. Their parents were helping them by sending money every month. They were living with friends who were already juniors or seniors and knew the ropes. They were in a sorority that practically guided them right through this tough college phase. They didn't have to do their own laundry, cook their own meals, work while going to school, none of that. At least that's the crowd I found myself in when I jumped into the sorority life, and I felt so out of place. I was a scrappy, tomboyish little fighter who really had no place joining a sorority. I just didn't know that at the time. I didn't know anything, other than I felt so entirely different and disconnected from everyone around me. I had just moved six states over and had driven my little beat-up Ford Escort, packed to the gills with my cheap, Wal-Mart-ish stuff, and hauled it all alone up to my new home, a dormitory room the size of two broom closets. I didn't know a soul, not even my pre-assigned roommate yet. I was bewildered.

But I was also, thankfully, brave and stubborn as hell. I had worked my ass off to get the grades, SAT scores, grant money, and the 5,000 dollars I'd saved hustling tips at a little Cracker-Barrel-like restaurant back home to get here, to go to college. To earn a better living than my parents did so life would be easier. I couldn't really tell you then what I wanted to do with my life, what I wanted my days to look like when I grew up. (Sadly as students, we are often just shuffled through the "this is what you're supposed to do" pipeline without giving a single thought

to how we might actually want to spend our time as adults.)
All I knew was that I wanted to earn a good salary so I didn't
have to live paycheck-to-paycheck like my parents did. For some
reason that was the ultimate goal. It no longer is. Money is now
an infinitely-less important commodity than my time (and my
health, which I still have, thank the fucking stars above!). But,
at the time, that was the goal. Go to college. Graduate with a
degree. Get a high-paying professional job. Get married, have
kids, a nice house, all that crap. That way you'll be sure to be
happy. *Because happiness is guaranteed if you do those things,
right?* Wrong. But that's an entirely different book.

At the time, I felt that I was supposed to study hard through
college, work to pay my tuition and room and board, so I could
get a degree and get a high-paying job and then life would
be easy. But, it was frustrating to have to keep telling myself
this, being my own cheerleader all the time, when everything
seemed for everyone else so easy. I found myself immersed
daily in old south money, college kids with fat monthly stipends
from their folks, brand new cars they were given as graduation
gifts, and the annoying blonde bitches with the intestine-less
waists and big, bouncy boobs. My god they were beautiful. And
all too perfect. It made me a little scared to be honest, that
life for me was just always going to be harder because I wasn't
perfect, and I had a Care Bear tummy.

But, I did have one thing under control; I was happily taken.
Back-Home Boyfriend—who had left our home state the same
time I did but traveling the other way, west to go to college in
San Francisco—and I were going to beat the odds! We were
going to be *that couple* (that one couple) that did the long
distance thing and did it well. We were going—both of us young,
wide-eyed, sexually excited and (while my mind didn't know it

at the time) both pretty damn smart, witty and good-looking—
to stay in a long-distance relationship, a long, long way apart
(cross-country) for a long, long time. Until we both graduated
and could get back together and be blissfully happy once again.
*Because that's how that works, right?*

But here's the problem. We were both a catch. Easily over any
one of the blonde bimbos and frat daddies at my school, at
least, because we could actually carry a conversation that didn't
involve football, pageants, or eight-point deer; and because we
were both very independent, motivated, and driven. I couldn't
say that about half the people I went to college with. Walk
around long enough as a catch in a place where everyone is
casting nets and sooner or later, you're going to get caught.
While I was propositioned on occasion, I truly believed Boyfriend
and I could do it. I truly did love him, as much as my young,
naïve heart could love anybody. (And I thought for years after,
it was more than I would ever be able to love anyone again,
because I now know how intensely painful it is to have your
heart broken.) I can tell you I never loved my husband the way I
loved that boy in San Francisco.

But Boyfriend was caught first. Snagged by some Angela-
named-slut whom he'd already slept with—hence the slut
designation—by the time he told me, over the phone while I
was kneeling on my dorm floor crying.

And, at first, while it hurt so much to know I didn't mean
enough to him to not stick his dick into someone else, I honestly
thought at first he was asking for forgiveness so we could try
and fix things. I soon learned again how stupid I was.

Boyfriend was telling me about his transgression because he had already decided to dump me. He had already chosen her over me. Her? Whoever the hell she was. I never saw a photo, thank God, because it probably would've imprinted so deeply that I would've never been able to see anything other than her face when I looked in the mirror, during college at least.

While I can't remember the words he actually used, I do recall Boyfriend briefly describing her, as part of his apology: "I'm sorry. She's just a lot of fun to be around and I realized you and I both need someone near us. We were never going to be able to do this. Trust me, Callie, you're beautiful and amazing and you're going to meet someone there soon, someone near you, and you'll see it too. You'll be glad I gave you the freedom to explore it."

A pretty rational, very mature explanation and apology, right? And, a totally adult, realistic, accurate one. Boyfriend really was doing me a favor. No one can enjoy a four-year, thousands-of-miles apart relationship; and no budding young adult should even try to attempt it and limit themselves so drastically at a time when they're supposed to be meeting new people, dating them, sleeping with them, hurting them, and getting hurt by them. This is how you learn who you are. Boyfriend was totally right and helpful and doing the right thing, for both him and me. I see that. Now. But that is not at all what I saw then. I. Was. Crushed. The earth under my feet disintegrated and my mind instantly warped. The one word I'm sure he did not say when he was describing Angela-the-Slut was one that I, for whatever reason, implanted.

## SKINNY

All he said was "fun to be around" and somewhere in my well-on-its-way to being effed-up mind, I imprinted SKINNY. And he had even told me I was "beautiful and amazing." But, I didn't hear that at all. The only thing I took away from the conversation was that Angela-the-slut must be skinny. Perhaps I felt like it was the one thing about myself that I could change. If someone who said they truly loved me—*me,* the entirety of my personality, my mind, and my body, everything that makes me *me*—could now say they don't love me anymore and they don't want to be with me anymore, then I had to believe my horrendous body was responsible for this. He dumped me because I was fat. Honestly, in a weird way, I see now that I chose that answer in an effort to protect my bleeding heart. To tell it, *"It's wasn't you, it was her. Your betrayal-of-a-body."*

I made myself imagine Angela-the-slut's long, toned, not-at-all-cheesy legs wrapped around him. My guy. My boyfriend. The man that I first loved. She had delicate, thin arms, an exquisite flat stomach that barely wrinkled when she sat down. I never saw a glimpse of her but I had already built up in my mind why she must have won out. She was funny, beautiful and—most importantly—SKINNY.

The lampshade photo came back to my mind. Suddenly I wasn't recognizable as a girl anymore. I had the body of a pudgy boy. I was a refrigerator.

I needed to get skinny.

Almost as immediately as I pictured her beautiful, skinny brown body wrapped around him, my mind replaced it with mine and I saw white cellulitely legs heaving on him. A belly folded three times over, so deep my belly button was swallowed whole and it was so big it literally pushed him up off of me. Tiny little nothing tits falling sadly to the side. And my stupid beefed-up gymnastics arms making it look like he was banging Arnold Schwarzenegger. It was such a gross image. I sucked in and held my tummy tight all day. I was so angry at it! It was like it all became so clear why I lost him and what I had to immediately take control of.

*You want skinny? I will murder skinny.*

Here's the thing, though: I was nowhere near fat. I don't think I suffered from the body dysmorphic syndrome folks talk about when they show a holocaust-looking teenage girl, her bones painfully prodding through her skin, staring at herself in the mirror and seeing a girl who is just pleasantly plump. I definitely went back to that lampshade moment in my mind and started generating some kind of body morphing disorder. Mine, though, wasn't that I was actually skin-and-bones but that I only saw pudgy. No, I just couldn't stand the look of my own body. My disgusting three-rolled tummy, my huge muscular monster thighs, my boxy frame making me look very little like a Victoria Secrets model from my shoulders down to my waist and very much more like a box freezer. I just hated the way that I looked. I hated my shape. I hated my lack of shape. And it had to be because I was fat. But, it would take years, many years, and many pounds both off and on to make me finally see that the things I don't like about my body—a bulky muscular core, meaty thighs, and a very short torso—are things that cannot be changed by losing weight. If anything, it only highlights them. They are structural issues, completely unrelated to how much extra flab I carry, or do not carry. But at the time, I would never be convinced of that. Boyfriend had dumped me because I wasn't pretty and skinny enough (that had to be the answer), and I was going to fucking change that. Because I could change that. I needed to change that.

I was so mad. But not at him. Here's the absolute wild thing: I was mad at me. Furious at me for being so hideously-ugly he had to dump me. I was going to punish me. *You want to be fat and ruin this life for me you degenerate body? I'll show you.*

I even baffle myself sometimes looking back on it and truly unraveling my actual, honest, very-harsh-in-the-daylight feelings. But the fire was lit. The seed was taking root and growing rapidly. And now I was living on my own. I could control what I ate, and far more importantly what I did not eat. It was the last few weeks of my first year in college. Yes, high school Boyfriend and I had made it almost nine months. We were very much in love, and he did cut me to the absolute core. And now—with the plan of going back to my home state to work during the summer and spend a blissful few months with him having been torched with a single phone call—I had to come up with a new plan. I felt alone. Hurt. Ugly. And out of control. The only way I believed I could prevent something like that from happening again was to establish and maintain complete control of my body, to not cut it any slack, not give it any breaks, and never give up the reigns. That's what I needed to do.

I wasn't really sure what that meant or how I was going to accomplish it, but I knew a switch had been flipped. I had changed. I had hardened. And I was ready to take all of my hurt out on something. I will regret to this day that the "thing" I chose to take it out on was my own body, but that's what I did. It started when I saw the second photo. Instantly, all of the wires in my brain snapped their old connections, frayed apart, and slowly began inkling back toward one another and re-connecting where they shouldn't. My re-wiring had begun.

**CHAPTER FOUR**

# BREAKFAST IS FOR PUSSIES: MY ANOREXIC PHASE

I remember the exact thought that went through my mind when I saw it: *Unlovable.*

I am 100% serious. I was eighteen, smart, attractive, well on my way to being successful. And because I was literally only fifteen pounds over my ideal weight, and because I saw a spring break picture from that year, my first in college, of me sitting on the beach in a bikini—I was pasty white and my stomach rolled and bulged over when I sat down—I was just that: unlovable. Why hadn't I curled my arms around my triple-rolled lump tummy or hid it some other way with a towel or magazine? *"At least suck in, you fattie!"* I screamed at my photo-self. I was mad at myself for letting that bowl full of jelly roll out. Then there was the real kicker in that photo: My skinny friend next to me, whose stomach was long, slender and flat. A lingerie model's tummy. The worst it did was cause three cute wrinkles in her skin when she leaned over. As if there wasn't a single ounce of fat on *it*, or *her*, anywhere in that photo. Her tummy wrinkles were like a bunny sneeze compared to the 7.0 Richter scale quake that was set off when my tectonic rolls collided. I know now, unwinding it all back in my mind, that while Boyfriend's shocking and hurtful dump planted the idea for my new cause—*I need to get skinny*—that second photo became the propaganda poster for it—*THIS is why. You're fat and unlovable.*

While it wasn't a very flattering picture—yes I was hunched over, which meant, yes, my stupid belly consisted of three bulging rolls that completely swallowed my belly button—there were two things I refused to believe when I saw it: 1) it was not (in any way, not even close!) the reason my boyfriend let me go; and 2) it was not something I would ever be able to change. That's just how my stomach looks, even when I'm super skinny, even when I'm super healthy and at my ideal goal weight, and even when I'm as I was there, maybe fifteen pounds over … maybe. I just have a lumpy tummy and always will. I know that *now*, but my God did it take years of punishment and torture followed by more years of forgiveness and revelations to get there.

Don't be me. Take the short-cut.

If there is a part of your body that you hate, that is fueling your food abuse and addiction, your dangerous, exhausting habits, ask yourself this: Has all of your starving and exercising, binging and purging made that part look better? If you lost a lot of weight and got to a point you *knew* was too skinny, did you feel confident enough then to go traipse the beach with that part hanging out? Was it still ugly in your mind? And, isn't that the same <u>insert your body part here</u> that you had when you were five? When you were twelve? When you were twenty? Has your entire life, every single year before you developed an eating disorder, really been so terribly awful, because of that dreadfully-hated part, so much so that it required some form of self-punishment? *I hate you Self! You deserve to be punished because you caused this!* And, most importantly: Whatever your "this" is (lack of self-confidence, dissatisfaction with your body, stress from your job, unwanted attention and pressure, disappointment, fear of failure, <u>insert your problem here</u>), has your eating disorder helped cure it? Did you just throw up your problems and suddenly they all went away? *"Bye-bye Lack of Self-Esteem. I'm Sasha Fierce now!"* Flush.

Of course not. In fact, it's probably worse *because* of your eating disorder. Now you might be even fatter, or even uglier (with a skinny, disproportionate body) than the person who stood before the mirror the moment you decided your body was to blame, so food must become the enemy.

That's exactly what I decided when I saw the spring break photo. It was about a month or so after I was dumped. While I had definitely, since the crushing blow, been avoiding anything that felt like junk food (cake, doughnuts, fried chicken, pizza, etc.) in a half-assed effort to start trying to get skinnier, I instantly decided it wasn't working and there would be nothing half-assed about it anymore. That's right. I'm committed dammit!

And combined with this commitment (an unfortunate recipe that only helped kick-start my sickness), was a new living situation that afforded me further control over my diet with less scrutiny. Because my "go back home to the boyfriend" plans were nixed, I decided to move in with my Dad in Alabama my first summer of college, to take extra classes and work and save until my second year. My Dad, a fantastically-funny and good-humored guy, is also a very hard worker, and he was often out making big rig cattle runs, managing his other businesses, or helping at the stockyards with cow sales and such. My point is our schedules didn't allow a lot of time together, particularly during meal time, as I was taking summer college classes during the day and waiting tables at night. This unfortunately left me with: 1) my own money to spend on food; 2) complete autonomy over my intake; and 3) a roommate/family member who had never, and probably would not until it became dangerous, commented on the appearance of my body—be it too fat or too skinny. Their daughter's weight is just not a topic many dads are ever going to happily broach. Which meant, for three months, I was left fairly free to deprive and torture myself with disgusting results.

I began absolutely refusing myself any indulgence when it came to food. *Breakfast? Are you kidding, you fat cow? Shut those stupid grumbles up with a stick of gum and get to class.* My hunger began to fuel me. I spent a lot of time studying and working out and ate the most ridiculous nibbles of food when I started to feel faint. A sliced tomato, chopped celery, a pack of crackers, a weightloss bar … Oh my! I silenced my hunger pangs with multiple cups of coffee (with calorie-free sweetener and fat-free creamer, of course) in the mornings. No breakfast. Never. *"Breakfast is for pussies!"* Then some eighty-calorie nothing-bar drowned by can after can of Diet Coke. Ahhh … Diet Coke. The magic wonder drink that fakes your body into feeling full and goes nowhere but back out. *Bloody genius!* Any healthy three-course meal was to be avoided because my body didn't deserve it. I was probably putting away about 600 to 800 calories a day, if I had to guess.

And—no surprise here—the weight quickly started to fall off. You know, those ghastly extra twelve pounds I was carrying. *For shame!* I could start to feel areas of my body that felt different than they had before. There was a divot behind my clavicle that started to feel taut and closer to the bone. I used to reach one hand to the opposite shoulder while studying (not eating, never!) and stroke this area to remind my starving body that I was losing fat. *We're almost beautiful and skinny. Hang in there!* As a very old, long-standing habit I still find myself stroking that area on occasion when I'm reading or deep in thought and finding myself so freaking grateful that it doesn't feel that way anymore. It was a sign my bony prominences were beginning to protrude and I never want that to happen again.

For me, it started with anorexia. Bulimia did not come until later, but it unfortunately lasted infinitely longer; because it's surprisingly far more easy to maintain and it's way more gratifying and rewarding. Sound twisted? Trust me, I am fully aware. But, I would be lying if I said there was never a time I missed that first greasy bite of a Whataburger Patty Melt on grease-soaked Texas toast, three juicy patties and four savory slices of cheese. Holy shit. Orgasm in my mouth. Are you suddenly starving right now?

You see? It's a hard habit to kick. But one that must be conquered, hopefully more easily than you realize. One of the worst down-sides I experienced while having an eating disorder control my life was the strain on friendships (or severance of them entirely), the damage to family, and the loss of time. So much freaking time I could have spent doing a thousand other more enjoyable (in no way shameful), healthy, memorable things. And here's the kicker: spend your time doing those things without an unnatural, overwhelming focus on food and you'll likely find yourself even *more* beautiful and well-proportioned than when your days were filled pushing people, invites, and opportunities away so you could be alone to squat over and shield your eating disorder from the world.

Ahhh ... but that is now. Let's get back to then.

Then I was starving myself, taking in far too few calories each day—not putting in enough energy and nutrition to fuel a hamster—and I began losing weight. *Take that Boyfriend! You too, Angela. You slut!* That disgusting image of me as a fat Schwarzenegger humping my boyfriend started to fade and my self-esteem began to rise. I was getting skinny! *Hell yeah!* People were complimenting me on how svelte I looked. I found that starvation really wasn't that hard, particularly when food was now my sworn enemy (and I'm a stubborn little fighter), and I could turn to the side and suck my tummy in and almost look exactly how I wanted. *Beautiful and skinny! Finally!* It was an awesome three weeks.

Then I got too skinny. Then even skinnier than that. Then grossly skinny. That was a weird six weeks. As you can imagine family members who were becoming increasingly more aware of my bird-like eating habits and starting to see my cheekbones and ribs jut out were not pleased and these conversations never went well. *Don't try to tell me what to do. I'm in control of everything here. Can't you see? Don't my flat ass and falling britches convey that?*

But, as I mentioned, thankfully I never seemed to form the type of bones-sees-buxom dysmorphic disorder, because I could see very well how sickeningly skinny I was. I never wanted to look uglier. And, I stupidly got a very short haircut around that time that made matters so much worse. Where once my blond hair had cascaded around my shoulders, unbeknownst to me, hiding those smooth little bone pockets on my clavicles, now a short hairdo brought everyone's eyes right to my jutting cheekbones and crane-like neck. It was bad.

Fights with the family erupted and I was glad to be heading back to school soon where I could get away from my taunting family members who kept trying to get me to eat all of their repugnant carbs, fried foods, and other fats. I was so stubborn. I never let a single morsel of anything that could be considered remotely "junk food" pass my lips. Cake, ice cream, doughnuts, cookies, pizza, hot dogs, burgers, fries, anything fried, chips, even regular, good-for-you carbs like potatoes, pasta, grains got the boot. *My body will turn every bite immediately into fat, don't you understand?* I was so excited to be out of their clutches and unforgiving glares and on my way back to skinny land where the bitches knew what it took to look good.

Except I didn't look good. Not at all. I looked like a starving, sick chemo patient. Bags had started to form under my eyes and my skin turned grey and lackluster. Little patches of my hair were falling out, but this is the first time I have mentioned that to anyone. Then it happened.

I got that look of: *"She must be sick in the head."* Because I mean why would you go to such great lengths, working so hard to not eat when your body needs it, and working out more than anyone should to look ... like shit? Like a nasty grey skeleton draped over a hanger. Why, on earth, would you do something that feels so much like punishment in an effort to look *good* when all it really does (if you would just snap to and look in the mirror and finally see) is make you look *bad*. Like you're sick and wilting.

What they don't tell you about dieting is that when you go overboard and refuse your body the nutrients it needs, sure you lose weight, but you also lose skin elasticity and color. You lose hair. You lose what were once attractive, healthy breasts. They become hanging sacks of sand. You also lose energy, patience, and joyfulness because you're so freaking hungry all the time. Many anorexics become isolated and mean (a) because they look too unhealthy to hang out with normal people without everyone trying to feed them all the time, so nix the friends. Then (b) they snap immediately at the mere mention of food, particularly at the people closest to them (family and friends) but it is the only topic that can reasonably come up when you are a hanging sack of skin. The many, many losses that come with you deciding to lose the healthy desire to eat food will haunt you more than the lost weight.

I was able to do it somewhat in solace because it was over a summer that I lived with my father and his girlfriend. Dads don't like to get into any girly stuff, so my withering-away was not a subject he was likely to bring up, and when his girlfriend tried, I snarled and snapped so fast and fierce she vowed never to try to help me with anything again. And I in no way blame her. I was snappy and vicious, because I was hurt, scared, and starving.

When it came time to start my second school year—thirty credits in and thirty pounds down—I moved into my first rental house in college well before my roommates. I didn't even let any of my family members help me move that day because I knew we would have to eat at some point (God forbid!) and that would put me in a food jam. So, I hauled all of my clothes, bedding, and furniture in my dad's horse trailer to the university and started to move in. My roommates, were friends from my freshman year and it had been two months (and two inches off every part of my body) since I had seen them. Because they would not be moving in until later in the week, I was able to get settled in before anyone—who knew me the previous semester as a happy, gregarious, normal college student—had yet to see me as the hollowed, cancerous-looking creature I had become. I started to get settled into the rental house and decided, as you often do after moving into a new place, that I needed all kinds of house-holdey type stuff: trash cans, paper towels, towel racks, organizer bins. So, I went to Wal-Mart and was wrestling a pretty hefty cart around when I heard her voice.

"Caaalllllie?" she asked, long and slow, sounding as if she was almost hoping it wasn't me.

I turned around. It was one of my sorority sisters, Erika. We'd had a pretty good time partying it up at the sorority/fraternity swaps the year before. I had even helped shuffle a few following frat puppies her way because I was so smitten with Boyfriend (that bastard!), but also because I was a healthy, beautiful blonde who was funny and easy to talk to. I had attracted a lot of college guys that first year, although I couldn't allow myself to remember any of that when I was a *"fat cow who'd been dumped."* Well, I wouldn't be attracting any boys now.

Erika's eyes went up and down over my shockingly-scrawny body and she then asked quite loudly: "What happened?"

I was baffled at first. I mean, I knew she was probably a little surprised that I'd lost some weight and was skinnier, but what did she mean by what "happened?" *I finally decided to stop being fat, that's what happened.*

I was kind of dumbstruck and asked her, "What do you mean?"

Then her eyes met mine and they said the words she couldn't: *"What kind of a person would do this to themselves? What kind of crazy she must be?"*

I'm grateful now to Erika because she didn't try to hide her disgust, didn't try to pretend like I looked normal, like this was all something we could pretend hadn't happened and I was still worth hanging out with. No. Erika made it very clear that if this was something I had chosen to do to myself, if *this* was the way I wanted to look to the world—like a bag of sick, sad bones—then I wasn't someone she wanted to spend her time with. I was so freakishly-thin I was ugly and I'm sure the thought of trying to just hang out with me, go to the movies, go shopping, go grab a stupid burger, would be all kinds of weird and uncomfortable because I abhorred food and I might faint in the next five minutes. She probably saw me as a liability. Someone she didn't want to be standing next to when I had my anorexic heart attack. Then she did the best and worst thing possible for me.

"You ... " she started in. "You look ... " but then her eyes caught mine and she could see that I very clearly did *not* see what it was she saw—a hollow-thin, anorexic girl.

My eyes probably conveyed confusion. *"I look what?"* they asked. Then she did it.

She laughed.

Not outright, but a quick little knee-jerk chuckle. Because it probably was a bit amusing to her to think I honestly had no clue how horrid I looked. *"What? You can't count each of your ribs, too?"* She laughed at me because I was a joke. The fact that I had gone to such self-inflicted lengths to make myself look repulsive all in an effort to be attractively skinny was—she had struck the very heart of it—laughable.

Erika quickly realized her chuckle was what cut the deepest and she immediately bumbled her way out of any more obligatory awkward conversation with me, because that's what any conversation with me would've been at that point. I was so alarmingly skinny that the only thing anyone could rightfully do when talking to me would be to try to get me to laugh big enough so they could shove a whole meatloaf into my mouth. That is the only thought that could have possibly crossed your mind when talking to me then.

Because I was a joke.

"I hope you get better," Erika mumbled and just pushed her cart away.

I will never forget that moment. I instinctively reached over and touched my clavicle, now no longer just a smooth pocket, but a bony protrusion. I had completely distorted myself. I used to be filled out. I used to have pink lips, a bright complexion, long flowing blonde hair and boobs. They weren't much, but they were enough to dance around and have some fun with. I used to have fun. I used to eat Oreos every once in a while and it was fine. It was fucking fine! Now I was a thin grey wisp of the vivacious, strong, lively person I used to be. I started crying. Not drops bowling over and falling out. No matter how messed up I was physically, I was still stubborn and strong and I was not going to be the sick girl crying at Wal-Mart. But, my eyes definitely welled up. Tears formed that I brushed away. I felt a wave of embarrassment wash over me and I prayed no one else I ever knew would ever see me like that again. I tried to think of how I could fix it. Overnight. Surely I could put on ten pounds in a couple of days, hiding in my room alone. My mind raced but I had a plan.

I grabbed a ball-cap off a shelf and walked as fast as I could without attracting too much attention toward the food aisles. "*Peanut butter,*" was my first thought. I remember realizing for the first time, when I started freaking out about how many calories and carbs food had, that peanut butter (something I used to love and enjoy occasionally in high school on crackers or bananas as part of a normal, *healthy* lifestyle) had like 100 calories per tablespoon. *Per tablespoon?!* For that reason, it had been instantly banned from my anorexic menu but now (*now?!*) I thought it would be the perfect solution. "*I'll eat a whole jar!*" I told myself as my eyes darted around, finally finding that wonderful shelf with the brown jars and red lids. JIF had always been my favorite.

*Choosy anorexics choose JIF!* What, not funny yet? It needs to be. This is an emotional roller coaster for a reason. At least ride it with me. It will help with the very hard "Stop doing this to yourself!" process that I hope is coming for you later. Trust me. *Once you can start to laugh about it* ... remember?! You cannot miss my peanut butter days!

I grabbed a jar and read the back. Two tablespoons equated

to 190 calories. *"We'll make it 200,"* I thought, for easy math. Twenty-four servings in a jar. A small jar. I grabbed the family size. Forty ounce. Servings per container: thirty-five. I did the quick math, 35 x 200 = 7,000 calories. *"Sweet!"* I thought. Couple of these jars and I'll at least look a little more normal by tomorrow. I won't scare people away. And I'll work my ass off to make sure this protein goes to the right places. I grabbed two jars. Then a third for good measure and had the lady at the register ring up my cap, too, so I could hide under it on my way to the car. I'm sure the poor gal thought I was some kind of food sicko, a bag of bones wobbling in front of her, buying three jars of peanut butter. She probably thought I was going to slather it on someone I had strung up in my basement, because that's how crazy I looked (and likely acted).

But I was going to turn shit around!

I hope you're starting to see a pattern for a lot of things here. When something in my life goes wrong, and I feel embarrassed, hurt, or angry about it, my knee-jerk reaction is often to blame myself for it. *"This likely happened because you were too stupid, fat, or ugly to prevent this from happening, right? Right, Callie?!"* I then immediately begin to punish myself with extreme forms of whatever it is I think I hadn't done enough of to avoid this nasty situation (study for hours, workout for even more, or starve myself for a day) thinking I can control things. *I can turn things around!* And, I often go off the deep end when I do because I'm a control freak, and the minute I feel I don't have it, I take wild, extreme (often ineffective) measures to try and get it back. Extreme diets, painful routines or exercises, even more painful bouts of hunger. It takes a serious kind of stubborn person to willingly inflict such harsh demerits on oneself. I can tell you this: anorexics and bulimics are the exact opposite of lazy. We are crafty, cunning, and relentless in our efforts to continue and hide our disorder. If you're trying to help a chronic bulimic, know that. Our will-power can level mountains, and we never give up.

I had seriously been planning on eating all three jars in one sitting that night. I was sure I could make myself do it.

I made it through one and a half.

To this day, I'm still a little proud I was able to put down even one complete forty-ounce jar in my first sitting. *The whole jar!* I know that's totally twisted, but sometimes when you look back on the stupidest shit you ever did, a little part of you wants to give your old self a fist bump, then follow it up immediately with a *"But never do that again, okay?"* I mean, a whole freaking family-sized jar? Do you know how much saliva it takes to get that sticky stuff down? It was good, too; delicious, intoxicating for the first ten spoonfuls, then it was hell, but I fought it down. Spoon after spoon. A jar and a half. That's like 10,000 calories in one sitting. While it in no way crossed my mind at the time (*"Shut up, Mind, I've got some body mending to do."*), looking back now, I wonder if 10,000 calories at once could stop your heart? Maybe. I'm sure it's digestion overload.

And, boy was I sick. I felt like I had a brick in my stomach for two days. Of course it didn't fix my "I gotta put twenty pounds on quick" problem, it just made my stomach protrude like a hungry Ethiopian kid while the rest of my features remained jutty and bony. Recall it was my bulging stomach that I hated to begin with. This went on for about a week—me forcing at least one jar of peanut butter down a day, mixed in with things I found made it easier to swallow (oatmeal, cream of wheat, smoothies, etc.)—thankfully with no one in the house with me. The roommates weren't moved in yet and Erika had been the only one, so far, to see me. I had massive stomach aches, turds so hard and callous I had to grip the counter and grunt to get them out. But, I did put on just enough weight—probably ten pounds if I had to guess—in that week to look a little bit more normal. Some color came back to my cheeks. I had so much energy I was often rosy and sweating just a little, which, at least was an improvement from my previous grey and pallid presence. While I did notice some mushiness coming in around my stomach and thighs (where weight always goes first on me), the boobs were filling out a little, which was a welcomed result. Overall, I knew I had gotten too thin. Erika's face when she saw me was appalling. I hadn't meant to get ugly-thin, scary-skinny, Ethiopian-style "I hope you get better" thin. I was only trying to get pretty-thin, boyfriends-wouldn't-dump-me-anymore thin. Well it would be a long time, decades, before I could figure out exactly what that meant for me and how to maintain it in a healthy way.

Now, I still think food is often the enemy, or at least an element of my life I have to watch with a close eye. Anything considered "junky" in my mind (pizza, hot dogs, ice cream, doughnuts, cookies, that kind of stuff) isn't even worth eating, or if it is, it needs to be a highly-justified and earned indulgence—which, all told, is not a terrible policy. I eat far more salads, vegetables, and lean meats now than probably most people my age, while in part as a choice to eat healthy, but also out of an unfounded-fear of eating too much of anything with bad fat and carbs. Eventually this lead to a very manageable, mostly healthy diet, which was great. That was years later, however. At the time, I had another problem.

I was addicted to peanut butter.

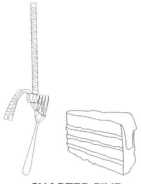

**CHAPTER FIVE**

# PEANUT BUTTER BLISS: MY BINGE-EATING PHASE

More accurately, I became addicted to the blissful feeling of stuffing myself, of eating past that point where I was perfectly satiated, even beyond the point of just full, to a point where I fell asleep from the sheer exhaustion of eating and slept incredibly hard because my body had so much work to do to digest all of the food I had just eaten. It was the most sound sleep. It was like eating my vicious, snarling mind away. Stuffing my face seemed to become one of the only ways I could quiet the angry beast within. Unfortunately for me, I discovered the sweet serenity of binging and my binge item of choice (the worst possible) was peanut butter.

I have told many people with whom I've shared this story that I honestly envision heaven as a place where I can eat a jar of peanut butter every day: JIF creamy, the low sodium version.

(With no rational tie to the sodium level, because that matters *none* when you eat a whole jar.) No, for some reason the low sodium version is firmer and has a little salty finish that I love. But, the ability to eat peanut butter all day—okay, and the occasional greasy burger, greasy cheese quesadilla, greasy burrito (man, grease is good)—would be the definition of heaven to me.

*Whoever's listening up there, if we could make that happen for Callie and others with eating disorders, that would be great. Just one jar a day is all I ask, with a big heavenly spoon. (And, of course the consumption of the peanut butter has no effect whatsoever on whatever angelic form I have. Even as angelic amorphous blob, I still need to be skinny and beautiful. Obviously.)*

But, during that turn-around period—when I was trying to pack weight onto my shriveled little frame—I LOVED eating a jar of peanut butter every day. And, it was a good thing I spent the miserable previous months starving myself because it at least afforded me those few weeks when peanut butter was exactly what my body needed. But, it was short-lived. As with any weight loss or gain, yo-yo-speed is not the best way to do it. Squishy pounds began to pack on and I filled out pretty quickly, primarily in the thighs and tummy area, which is where all my fat goes first. *Bullocks!*

So then I tried to get back to eating normal. Before college, I was a gymnast, a cheerleader, a very active, healthy person. And I ate a lot. You can do that when you're eighteen and active and it doesn't have much of an impact. I distinctly remember going to Olive Garden on one varsity road trip in high school and eating five of those warm buttery breadsticks—each bite dipped in

Alfredo, naturally. This was before my meal even came. And I had ordered pasta! Back then I could eat pasta. You know, without thinking about it. That was pretty par for the course for me then. But, I was also super active and I ate normal. Some days I would eat light and perfectly healthy just because it was the food that was put in front of me. I didn't really think about it. Then other days, I would eat heavy—tons of bread, cheese, and pasta, simply because it was the food that was put in front of me—and I didn't really think about that either. Food was not an obsession then, which meant food was not a problem then.

But because I ate heartily and I have a naturally-stocky build, when I began college I was a pretty stout gal. I probably carried an extra ten pounds I didn't need, but they were not in any way detrimental. I likely could have maintained that weight my entire four years in undergrad and enjoyed my meals and focused all of my food-obsessive energy on much greater feats. Instead, I chose to punish myself with horrendous starvation periods, followed by massive binges—where I would again eat an entire jar of peanut butter, then curse my fat, ugly body and cry. *Why did I do that for so long?*

The only answer I can come up with is because I was sick. I had warped and re-programmed my mind and I couldn't see the reality of what I was doing. That black gnarly vine that was my eating disorder was twisted so tight around my psyche that I did not see any other option. Food became both the luscious carrot at the end of the stick and the stick itself, slapped at me like a whip when I thought about just eating a normal meal. *Why did I do that for so long?* Sometimes, I tell myself perhaps I was meant to endure it to become this voice and help others. Whether or not that's true, it at least helps me forgive myself for the repulsive and horrible things I did to my amazing body for so, so long.

When I honestly try to dissect it all and figure out what the hell happened—why I became so abnormal by choice—I believe it was an accumulation of life stressors. First there was the immense stress of starting an independent adult life alone. When you don't know what lies ahead, how difficult or costly it might be, and whether it will even afford you the life you really want to live if you are able to attain it, needless to say your confidence is shaken. This is amplified when you're thrown into a vat of people you feel are more privileged, prettier, or capable than you. And they all seem so fragile and feminine, sculpted by a steady hand into the demure, elegant, voluptuous frame that women are supposed to have. For me, fitting none of those descriptors (in my mind) was unnerving. *"If I am competing alongside these perfect creatures for the same things— recognition, success, love, happiness—surely I will lose because I don't seem as deserving as they do."*

I know these thoughts sound very silly, *now*. Now that I am a grown woman, fully confident in my own abilities and attributes, but I was not that woman then. And, to this day, my self-confidence changes as frequently as the weather. Some days I feel like Sasha Fierce on the catwalk; other days I feel like old, blubbery, refrigerator Callie, with a lampshade on her head. I just simply know now how to better cope with my refrigerator days and how to kick myself out of my own funk; and food has nothing to do with that process. Food is no longer a punishment tool. Food is no longer the enemy. But, looking back, I believe that can be the formula for many to plant the seed and begin nurturing their own eating disorder: stress, fear, uncertainty, and a lack of confidence. Drop one big, crushing bomb on top of that (such as the loss of a lover, a job, a place to live, a friend or loved one, a huge financial blow, or other failure) and it all crumbles like a house of cards. Then you're lying flat on a pile of pain and rubble and that seed starts sprouting, crawling through your skin, gripping the base of your brain and holding you down while whispering: *"This is your fault. You need to gain control and become different so this won't happen again."* Often that "different" is skinny.

Looking back, it reminds me of that stupid girl in the restaurant who cries and throws her fork when the waiter comes by, screaming: "My boyfriend thinks I'm fat!" What a snivelly little weakling. I could crush her. Yet, I have to admit that I was actually far weaker than her because, rather than letting some emotions out in public where they might be aired out, exposed, and cleared, I took mine home with me. I swallowed them and hid them. Fed them and grew them. I locked the door and hugged them like a toilet. I lived with my emotions on the inside, under a bulletproof, size-four suit. No one on the outside was ever allowed to see them because I chose to let no one else in. I was too afraid to try that again. *"People are not to be trusted. Food is to be used as a tool. And no one will ever hurt me again."* I had been blindsided and hurt (in my mind) because I was fat and ugly. And I made the very poor decision that I could "fix" everything by "breaking" my food programming.

Food was no longer just a form of sustenance, something necessary that needed to be consumed a few times a day, that should've been chosen wisely and taken in moderation, and *enjoyed*. For me, it became a form of torture that brought me immense pleasure and painful bouts of overwhelming guilt and shame. It was like a drug. I was definitely addicted. The thing that brought me the most physical pleasure was binging, but the thing that brought me the most intense mental anguish was feeling shame at the sight of my hideous, squishy body afterward and thinking it needed to be tortured back into shape. My starvation period started it, but my peanut butter period solidified it. I had royally fucked up my mental approach to food. It became both the enemy and the love affair. And, it would take years—more than a decade—for me to begin to approach food again with any form of trust.

I could no longer just eat. A burger. For wayward, re-wired Callie, the almighty in-and-out had taken over.

# RUN 'TILL YOU SEE STARS: MY EXERCISE-BULIMIC PHASE

Through seven years of college, then law school and my first few years in the practice (that's ten years total! *Ten?!*) I was on a food/weight rollercoaster. At times I would be twenty pounds down, looking rather svelte and able to feel that little concave area on my clavicle, but then the thought of that moment in Wal-Mart—when Erika looked at me with such horror—would flood back and I would tear into another jar of peanut butter. More often than not I was twenty pounds over, with fat squishy thighs that I would squeeze into pantyhose for work and legal functions, knowing exactly how overweight I felt and looked and hating myself for it. Food caused me such angst. *Should I* eat that? Should I eat three of that? "You shouldn't eat anything until tomorrow, you heifer!" my mind would shout at me. That mental soundtrack would begin to play well before any meal time and taunt me throughout.

And, the "Should I eat that? Don't eat that or anything else!" soundtrack is just half of the tape—Side A. Side B was the all-important "out." Just as strong and loud as my mental shouts over what to eat and when, were my resounding cries as to how I was going to get those nasty calories out. "Workout! Workout! Get it out!" my mind would cry. Unfortunately for me, there was an awesome, newly-constructed, four-million-dollar fitness center on campus that, as an undergrad student, I was free to use anytime I liked. I liked all the time. Every day. Once a day at least. Often twice. At least a hundred crunches before bed if I didn't make it to the gym. Every night back-to-back with no days of rest, which I can assure you worked wonders on my monster muscular gut by growing it into a thick bulky muscle. And once I began a rigorous exercise program, just like food, it became a daily unhealthy desire. Working out was not an activity meant to make me *feel* good and keep my body healthy, but solely to purge whatever forbidden calories I had previously put in. Exercise was my first form of purging.

I was so committed to it that if, by chance, my day somehow got too full or inadvertently cluttered that it appeared I would not be able to work out, I immediately panicked. I would get antsy and snarly if I had to go one day without working out. I was insanely committed to purging via exercise. I would do cardio until my ears popped. I lifted weights until I felt light-headed. Sometimes I ran so hard that I became incontinent. I pissed all over myself because I couldn't stop my bladder; she was so tired she threw in the towel. And once she did (because, yes, I saw her as a part separate from me), I ran even harder and further. Why? Because the only logical thing to do, then—when you're on the treadmill with a wet half-moon between your thighs—was to keep my legs moving to hide it until my leggings dried themselves. That, or I would have to run straight from the treadmill, out the front door, and home so people would not see that I had wet myself.

But Callie Wet Rally at the gym was not nearly the most embarrassing state I found myself in. Just wait. Callie turning strange colors is coming.

In addition to my excessively-insane workout regimen, my brilliant food plan at the time (my second and third years of undergrad) was to avoid anything with carbs or fat. Any fat at all. I was afraid of any package that boasted three grams of fat or more per serving. This meant my diet consisted mostly of canned vegetables with salt on them, fruits, salads (with fat free dressing, of course), lean meats (except I thought lunch meat was good for you), many cans of tuna with relish, etc. Obviously, I didn't cook. Obviously, most of my foods were processed or very high in sodium. And, obviously, this was not very good for my body. On top of that, I also still suffered the occasional had-a-bad-day binge, which resulted in a half-eaten jar of peanut butter (because fat no longer matters once you've decided to binge, only the satisfying release of stuffing yourself does).

And, as perverted as this sounds, I would only allow myself to binge on peanut butter. Nothing else with it. Straight up peanut butter. Because if I'm going to allow myself the very stupid, embarrassing *"You're such a weakling!"* binge in hopes of fixing my "bad day," then I'm going to make sure I remember next time how much that binge cost me when it sets me back 7,000 calories and 560 grams of fat in one sitting. Yes, one sitting. Why this particular form of torture upon torture? Because, even while binging, *"I'm still in control, bitches!"* Do you see how warped I was? It was a stupid diet. And a very counter-productive diet, if you want a body that is healthy and curvy and feels good. It also didn't taste very good and made eating out with friends, family, colleagues and co-workers rather difficult. I would only order the salad, always the salad. Then go home and eat out of cans. Until I found a new friend.

It was normalcy no more for Callie. Cue that yellow buttery goodness and my new phase: My Butter-Spray Days!

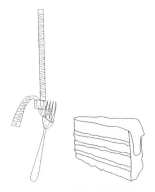

**CHAPTER SEVEN**

# NORMALCY NO MORE: MY BUTTER-SPRAY DAYS

I remember when I first saw it on the shelf at the grocery store. That heavenly yellow bottle. It claimed to look like butter, to taste like butter, yet have only one gram of fat—just a single measly gram—I was elated! *"Now my many, many cans of veggies and potted meats can actually taste good* and *still have almost no fat? Hell yeah!"* I was also stupid. I did not know then that if the portion is small enough—like, say, a single *spray*— then, sure, that one "ka-chook" spray can amount to only one gram of fat. This math no longer works, however, if you *pour* butter-spray on things, if you coat, douse, and drown them with it. Or, better yet, if you pour butter-spray in a dish and submerge things in it. Glub, glub.

It doesn't work if you consume a bottle or two of butter-spray a day.

I can't even begin to imagine now what the handful of roommates I had in college and law school thought of me. When I went to the grocery store, I would buy seven to eight bottles of butter-spray. One shelf in the door of my fridge (at several residences) was always devoted to range of four to eight bottles of butter-spray. I never even spritzed the shit. *"Ain't nobody got time for that!"* The lid was always unscrewed and the yellowy goodness dumped out.

You can imagine during this time I lost many friends. I freaked people out. I was also pretty snarly and mean if anyone ever remotely tried to touch on the subject of my indescribably-odd consumption of butter-spray, which in reality, was a comment on my now very-noticeable eating disorder. *"I don't know what you're talking about. I'm totally normal."* Except I wasn't. I was always eating alone, smuggling dishes back to my room, hiding my butter-soaked meal in a drawer, opening it to take a bite and closing it back up thinking no one would see the very weird thing I was doing to my body. But, they did. Everyone did. How?

My fingers turned yellow.

Then my entire hands. Apparently, if you glug a quart of beta carotene a day, it will do that. After a while it was hard to hide. I was unnaturally skinny (for my body type), I had very little body fat at the time, and the ends of my long, slender fingers were a noticeably-odd yellowish-orange. It was even more apparent when my hands were near or touching others' because of the stark comparison of healthy, plush pink to my sinewy yellow spindles. It also showed very well in photos when my hands were on that of a normal person. Basically, my skin had an overall orange glow to it, like an Oompa Loompa.

I'm not kidding.

My aunt, to this day when she sees me, will bring that up and say, "I'm so glad you're not *orange* anymore."

Well, I most certainly was then. It also didn't help that I was unattractively skinny. I hadn't reverted back to that waif Wal-Mart version of me, but I didn't have an ounce of fat on my body. Even with all the fat of the butter-spray, because I exercised for at least one hour every day. And with all that working out, all of that energy forged into pushing my body so hard and it didn't look good. I was skinny, but still with a protruding muscular gut (nothing will ever change that) and tight, little knotty muscles because the only fuel I would give my body was canned vegetables and tuna, all swimming in yellow margarine, probably a form of plastic, that isn't even real food. I'm sure it's recycled Barbie parts and cow blubber mixed with beta carotene. Some super-healthy formula like that. How was my body supposed to create anything beautiful with that? I'm damn lucky it even continued to stand upright. Better yet, that with all of that torture, it continued to work, study, excel, perform, and achieve.

I will spend the rest of my days thanking my body for sticking with me despite the years of horrendous torture I inflicted on it.

But this is now. That was then. At the time, I stupidly congratulated myself on having not yet gone to the dark side of throwing up after I ate. *"Sure, I can't approach food without counting the calories, torturing myself with the options, and planning to burn off whatever I put in afterward, but at least I don't do* that. *I'm not* that *far gone,"* I would tell myself. *"You're so smart, Callie."*

Was I? I was still starving at times. Putting away an entire jar of peanut butter at others—when my hunger, irritation, and impatience would overwhelm me, and in response, I would crash into the bottom of that brown, creamy hell. Heaven? Hell? I can't decide. Sadly, one very unfortunate side effect of even just a brief distortion of what food is and what it means to your body can, in some cases, never be undone. Once you see food as the enemy and decide—no matter how bad you crave it—it must be loathed, chastised, and purged, it's very hard to go back to "eating normal." Every calorie is mentally counted, every gram of fat, before the food item is ever ordered, purchased, or unwrapped, much less eaten then purged. "Grabbing a bite to eat," is no longer just part of a normal day. Whether to eat, when, how much, *what* you should eat—and, the most important factor: how you're going to get it out—is a thought process that torments every hour of your every day. I'm not kidding. The disorder consumes your thoughts. It's astounding—if you are one of the lucky ones who finally recovers and are able to look back and *see*—the enormous amounts of time you spent wasting on this very unnecessary aspect of your life when you could have used that time to paint a masterpiece, learn to tango, go to Bali, write a damn book, what-the-hell-ever-*else* besides counting and cataloging your input and output. It's exhausting. And totally and completely unnecessary.

I distinctly remember hearing another eating disorder survivor say how embarrassed she felt looking back and remembering one of the most important thoughts on her wedding day was how many calories she had taken in and how many she needed to purge out. On her *wedding day*. And, she's beautiful. She has the kind of body we imagine as we're sticking our fingers down our throats and heaving. It is called a disorder for a reason. Because it makes no rational sense. It's completely counterproductive and, the saddest part, it is also dissatisfying and damaging. The very outcome we all are trying to accomplish—a nice body—is the last thing that will come from re-wiring our body's response to food. Rather than taking it in frequently as healthy, necessary fuel, you teach your body (because you starve it for long periods) to store, rather than burn, what little you give her. Then, when you cave and binge (because we all have bad days and do that), your body savagely grabs whatever fat particles it can *first* and stores those, *first*, because it knows those will be the first to go when the starving begins again. So, despite all of this massive effort you are putting in, your body remains squishy and tired. Because it is!

To me, it seems a lot like sex. Something you should naturally crave, need, have, and *enjoy* in a frequent, healthy way suddenly gets perverted when it is used as a means of punishment, of power, of unhealthy pleasure. Once you've re-wired your need, desire, and entitlement to food, it is hard to just revert back and do it like normal, for the right reasons, at the right dose, at appropriate times because it has mutated into something different for you. The normalcy and healthy necessity of it has been stripped, leaving your desire and use of it perverted.

And, unfortunately, this often means that even if you eventually solve or overcome whatever initial problem triggered your eating disorder—a break-up, divorce, a career or financial stressor perhaps—and that aspect of your life is now mended, your food issues remain, because they are simply now part of your psyche, part of your every day. Am I going to binge today or not? You'll start to think about it when you wake up. Both the intoxicating pleasure of it, the burden of hiding it, and how you will somehow get enough sustenance to remain in your body that day to still feel skinny but not pass out, while you're waiting to do it. These are serious thoughts that circle through your brain on a conveyor belt, going round and round. Even on your wedding day. Perhaps *especially* on your wedding day, because that's a day you need to feel your most beautiful and skinny, right? Hope you don't get any vomit on that pretty white dress when you puke up your wedding cake. And it will probably be just the one mouthful that you will feel you need to purge because you unfortunately *had* to swallow it as part of that whole stupid smash-some-cake-in-each-other's-face bit. What an annoying food jam?! A cultural ritual that forces you to eat cake! On your wedding day?! As if you actually wanted to *eat* any of that damn cake. Well, keep it down rather. No matter how much you may want it, you can never keep any of it down. *Are you crazy? That shit goes straight to the thighs!*

But, secretly you know, banishing everyone from the reception hall, unzipping your dress, and sitting in the corner stuffing the entire cake in your mouth by hand, each heavenly-sweet, frosting-coated bite after another, would bring you far more pleasure than your husband ever could. I can guarantee you: any bride who is thinking about binging and purging on her wedding day derives more pleasure from food than from her spouse. I can say that because I've been married, while honing and hiding an eating disorder. Boy, was that frustrating? And exhausting. That's why it had to end.

The marriage. Not the eating disorder. *Are you crazy?* Don't worry. We'll get there.

By this time, I was in law school, studying very hard, while working a part-time job as a legal clerk, while keeping up a house and two dogs. Oh, and I was married. Yes, it does seem trivial compared to the huge salivating monster who lived in my head and whom I battled every day. I spent way more time fighting and soothing my monster than I did caring for my husband. But don't pity him; he had his share of bad traits, too. Now, we both know he and I were never meant to be bonded forever. We were just young and on a life-conveyor-belt and it was just a thing you did because you thought you were supposed to. First you date for a bit, then move in together, he proposes, you can only say yes. Boom. It's done. You're married. If only curing an eating disorder was that easy. Let's hope, with some hilarious revelations in here, it can be for you.

I was about a year into my butter-spray days, not quite yellow yet, when Husband and I met, and he soon after (because he did not have another place to stay) moved in with me. Since I was the sole breadwinner and well-established Head and Almighty Ruler of the House, Husband knew not to say anything about my weird eating habits or my weight at any time. And, what the hell did he care anyway? He was getting a free ride. We ended up getting married and the most prevalent thing on my mind that day, I can assure you, was the cake. While he was a decent enough guy, I was always thinking about my food intake, both my love and hate of it. So, I can easily stand by what I said before: Husband was never going to be able to bring me the kind of pleasure—or pain—food can.

Does that sound strange to you? That, for me, food could have more of an impact on my life than people did? Do you feel that way? That you care about food more than some of the people in your life? Perhaps *all* of the people in your life?

If you have not come to terms with that fact, please do now. Eating disorders are that powerful.

They are also stressful and time-consuming. It's amazing how highly-functional people with full-blown eating disorders can be; because on top of all our legitimate, real-life worries, we pile on top the far more important, constant worry about what to eat, how much to eat, whether to eat with people or in seclusion, how to hide what we're eating, and, even more importantly, how to extract what we've eaten. It takes a lot of inner strength to deprive yourself of food. The same kind that can make you study fourteen hours a day for college exams and the LSAT. The same kind that allows you to work your way through law school and pass the Bar Exam. It is the very nature of an eating disorder—*i.e.*, that it requires great mental fortitude to make yourself do incredibly difficult things to yourself, like starve or purge—that also makes us, often, very successful people. Bulimics, in particular, will often appear like people who have everything in their life under control. They will look to others like they are on top of their game, which they are. It's just ... the game is bulimia. I'll get into that soon.

For now, one good thing to come out of my marriage will be the end of my Oompa Loompa days. It was also the beginning of my bulimia phase. As I sit now and try to unravel it all and figure out why it really happened, why I intentionally and consciously chose this road, I truly believe it was because of two very changeable and manageable factors in my life. First, I was **stressed** (more stressed than I've been in my entire adult life) then **busy** (busier than I've ever been in my adult life). Combine those with the fact that I had a raging eating disorder—that food was not a means of health and sustenance for me, it was an everyday torturous problem, a perverted drug to either binge on indulgently or banish to the corner—and bulimia then seems like the easy answer.

And, I didn't want to admit I had a horrendous eating disorder because: a) it meant I was broken and needed fixing; or b) which is much closer to the truth (because I knew I was broken and needed fixing), I didn't have the time or luxury to put my busy life on hold to try to fix myself so I could recover from my eating disorder. Yeah, that's right. I didn't have the time to focus on my health, because I was too busy living a stressful, demanding life (a life that was only possible if I was alive and in good health). That's the smart person I was. But, because I truly believed these things and I truly felt this way, I also felt that it left me with only one choice. Onward and upward. What goes down …

So, let's start this journey. Take my hand, will you? *Don't worry, I washed it.*

## STRESS

If I could sum up my first year of law school in one word it would be intimidating. Knowing I was the gal who came from across the country to attend this college. The one who drove herself to the dorm to move in, alone. The one who paid her own college tuition and made her own way. But, that was all fueled by a terror that I wasn't going to be smart enough to, unlike my parents, get a degree, get the successful job, and get the big, fat salary. My ability to succeed was tied directly to my fear that I was not smart enough, which made me work two times harder than the student to my left and three times harder than the student to my right. And, in law school, where most of the students were, in fact, legitimately, smarter than me, this fear became overwhelming. In law school, everyone seemed so intelligent, like they had all the answers all the time, without having to do any work to conjure them. I often felt like I was the only one who was flustered and afraid. And, there was only one test at the very end of each course. Every single day of attending classes, reading, writing summaries, taking notes, making a tedious outline, and then studying said outline, all culminated to one three-hour test at the end of the semester where I had to write an essay that spouted back everything, correctly, that I was taught in that course. If not, I would fail. "Sorry you wasted the last five months."

It was utterly frustrating that very much *unlike* undergrad— where there were quizzes, midterms, papers graded, *feedback offered* throughout the semester where students could gage their abilities and what it was the professor wanted out of them, and, thus, adapt—in law school, it was one singular, unknown moment that determined whether you would succeed or fail. This setup, particularly for people who are hard-workers, diligent, and disciplined (bulimics, I know you hear me), was incredibly stressful; because without feedback letting us know we are on the right track, we cannot easily make ourselves stop studying. *"I don't know yet if I know this stuff well enough yet, so I must keep studying. Mustn't stop yet."* It was a very difficult, high-pressure couple of years for me. And intense stress is never good for someone with an eating disorder. While we usually always do manage somehow and push through, we don't have the best coping techniques.

Let my yellow fingers be proof. But, thankfully, after enough questions and odd looks from Husband, his family, my family, friends, co-workers, and fellow law students, my orange façade finally persuaded me to cut back on the butter-spray. Good for me. I had a real opportunity here, at a time in my life when I was exceedingly stressed and where recovering from my eating disorder and getting back to a healthy mind and body would have been the absolute best thing I could have done for myself, my future, and my body. But, I chose to do the opposite. Why? I believe it was because I was busy. Yep, I'm about to start throwing up my food because I'm busy. Makes perfect sense, right? To me it did. Let's go there.

After I decided to nix the yellow spray, I did *try* to start eating normal and healthy. At least what I considered healthy at the time. I often bought twenty packages of microwaveable Green Giant frozen veggie boxes at a time because I ate two or three of those a day, thinking they were a good vegetable going in. Who cared that I couldn't pronounce the ingredients in the sauce they were swimming in. *"It's got a picture of vegetables on the front and not a lot of fat listed on the back. And, I'm sure xantham gum is good for me."* But that, too, is laughable because I never read ingredients. *"Ain't nobody got time for that!"* I didn't even have time to look at expiration dates. I bought huge quantities of what I considered low-fat, low-calorie diet type foods that were either ready to eat hand-to-mouth, or could be ready in a few microwave minutes. Why? I'm busy!

## BUSY

In law school I had to work. I had been on my own financially since I started college and while the law school "frowned upon it" and encouraged students not to work so they could focus on their rather-difficult studies, there was no other way *my* bills were going to get paid. So, *c'est la vie.* I got a job as a legal clerk with a local law firm and I worked around my law school classes. And, as a law student, legal clerk, breadwinner not to mention lawn-mowing, grocery-shopping, house-cleaning wife, I was busy. Not only did I not know *how* to cook, I had no time to learn or buy anything with dirt on it that required cleaning, cutting, cooking, none of that. I was busy! Or so I thought. I had less time to work out in law school and I ate mostly packaged crap, all while still accommodating the occasional peanut butter binge when I performed poorly in class or at the firm, felt like I had asked a stupid question, felt like I had failed to interpret a case correctly and made a stupid comment in class, you name it. Anytime I didn't feel smart or capable enough, doubted myself, and had a bad day, it ended in peanut butter.

Do you see how hard I was on myself? While trying to learn and succeed in a very difficult study course and even-more challenging career, when I made a mistake there was no forgiveness, there was immediate punishment: a peanut-butter binge that would only leave me feeling more guilty, more defeated, and now literally fatter than I was before. I was horrible to myself. And, then, I was also taking more food in and working less off because I was busy and stressed. I looked like crap and my squishy, tortured, tired body reflected exactly what I was doing to it. I hated, loved, mostly hated, yet still loved food.

Looking back, had I just learned to nix the peanut butter binges and cook healthy meals then, in law school (when I had plenty of time), things might have turned around for me. I know *now* I had plenty of time to do it. It's not like it takes three hours every night (although I thought that at the time) to make a healthy dinner, and it's not like raw vegetables and meat are so daunting (which I also thought at the time). I could have easily spared thirty to forty minutes each evening to make a nice meal. Heck, it might have helped ease my overwhelming stress. I wasn't *that* busy. And, while it was also impossible (and unnecessary) to get the two hours every day at the gym I had been previously getting, I know *now* that two hours of exercise every day is counter-productive and bad for me and that I could have easily spared thirty to forty minutes every *other* day for a nice, moderate workout. Again, it might have helped tremendously with the overwhelming stress I was feeling. I wasn't *that* busy. But, you can never forget (although I would never acknowledge it at the time, that would take many more years) I was still damaged, re-wired, generally "messed up" when it came to food.

Although I was married at the time, my eating disorder, and the exhausting maintenance of it, was way more important to me. I'm divorced now, obviously, because I was mad at him. Mostly mad at myself. At the heart of an eating disorder is anger at oneself. We are mad at ourselves because we just binged, which makes us feel incredibly weak. Or we're mad at ourselves because we are trying so incredibly hard—eating rabbit food all day, swooning from hunger, and working out until we see stars—and yet it's STILL NOT WORKING. We're still fat and ugly (in our minds) and others around us are perfectly thin while eating cake. It pisses us off, so we continue to punish ourselves more. Our anger doesn't leave any room in our minds or hearts for a healthy, intimate relationship. Imagine my response when my husband wanted to have sex with me on a night when all I wanted to do was binge. Or, worse yet, after I just ate an entire pizza. If he reached out to touch me then I'm sure the look I gave him felt like a gripped hand on his throat lifting him off the ground. *"My body is to be hated. Not to be lovingly touched. Hands off, you!"*

These are real feelings we have. And they're so wrong, and they're so damaging, but we can't change them. This is how we *feel* and it's why we continue to do what we do.

But you can choose to live alone, fuming, pissed off, exhausted and ugly (yes, ugly, because your tortured body can be nothing else) until your death; or you can try to see what you're doing and change it. While I asked for and chose to get divorced for many reasons (some good and right, some not), I am a healthy enough person now to look back and see that a good bit of our tension derived from my eating disorder. If you are harboring an eating disorder, I'm sure the cracks in many of your relationships (if they haven't already been severed completely because they got in the way) can be traced back to your disorder, your anger, your decision to continue to treat your body this way.

It is going to take a long time, and you are going to slip, and you are going to have to forgive yourself often, and get back on the difficult track; but it will only start when you're ready to truly give it up: to eat normal, let people in, keep it all down, and see what happens. When you're finally brave enough to do that, everything will change. It will all get so much easier, you'll drop those hot, heavy bags of hate (for yourself) that you've been carrying around, and you'll be a much happier person. Had I realized that then, in law school, and made the conscious decision to finally fix my terrible eating habits and get healthy, my path would have taken a very different turn. But, was I ready to do that yet?

Nope. Not I! I was a busy law student, soon-to-become busier lawyer, needing to control everything in my life. While I hated the stress of my law school days, I had no idea what real stress was. As a young, practicing attorney, I worried myself to levels I never thought possible over whether I had failed to find and read a crucial document that was produced in discovery, whether I had asked an expert witness a necessary, case-dependent question in his deposition, whether I had performed satisfactorily enough to impress my partners so I could keep my job. I did not know at the time how much stress I was putting on myself and what that was doing to my body. But the change was visible. Because I spent most days hunkered over my computer typing, fretting, and typing some more, fat gravitated toward my midsection and congealed. I was becoming one of the many white pudgy elders I practiced with every day who— unfortunately due to a poor diet and lack of exercise, coupled with a stressful, sit-all-day job—had been saddled with spare tires. Their pasty, paunchy stomachs overlapping their belts, their only exercise routine a walk from the car to the door and back on weak, shriveled legs. They likely couldn't run a mile, much less a city block, even if a flood was coming. There are hundreds of millions of Americans just like this. This is who I was becoming.

I knew something had to change, because I was getting actual, real-life, "it's not just a vision in the mirror" fat. While I'm probably a size four, perhaps six, as a healthy version of Callie, I was an eight, trending toward a ten. Most of my suits had to be eights or tens or they would not button around my growing mid-section. While I tried to eat healthy packaged stuff, along with Diet Cokes and salad, I still suffered the occasional peanut butter binge when I'd had a terribly-defeating day, which meant my relationship with food was still very much warped. I still had an eating disorder. So I still had the same *"I'm in control here!"* mentality. Never, ever, would I allow myself to be ... *fat*. Never. No. Not an option.

But to make sure that didn't happen, something had to change. This was another cross-roads. At this juncture, as with the many before it, I could have easily done some research on healthy eating and exercise habits and started a new regimen. I mean, I am a freaking lawyer. I research much more complicated shit all day long. I'm not dumb. I also could have joined a gym, found a friend who wanted to make a healthy lifestyle change too and we could have done it together—any number of tactics that could have turned things around for me and ended this vicious cycle ten years sooner. But, no. I did not. I was still stupid, with a long, dangerous road of stupidity yet to travel ahead. Just like the day I saw that fat photo of myself at the beach, the day I opened my first soon-to-be-eaten-in-one-sitting jar of peanut butter, the day I bought my first bottle of butter-spray, I made another very poor decision. And please do follow this line of reasoning carefully with me, because if it is yours as well, I hope you will finally see the futility of it. Remember, food was the enemy. I was improperly wired and until that very fundamental problem was fixed, I could not just eat normal. I couldn't. While food had to go in (only so I didn't wither away and faint at my desk), every ounce of it needed to come out so I would stay skinny and powerful and in control. So here's what I came up with:

*"I don't have the time or energy to work it off, so I have to find another way to get it out."*

Yes, I had a law degree. I passed the Bar. I was a lawyer. Some people might have considered me a smart person at the time. Obviously they were wrong. I was an idiot. One who had been treating her body very badly for a decade now, virtually programmed to blame and rebuke her for any bad thing that happened to me, and one who decided to take it ten steps further and dole out punishment so horrendous no body should ever have to suffer it. Welcome to the bowl.

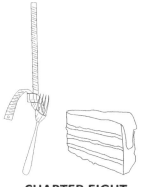

**CHAPTER EIGHT**

# FOOD IS NOW MY DRUG: MY FULL-BLOWN BULIMIA PHASE

I have spent a lot of time trying to tread back through all of this, a) so I could better understand it myself; and b) hopefully, be able to explain it in a way that translates it for those who want to just understand it to help others or who want to quit themselves. The urge is so, so strong. It is bliss, satisfaction, an intoxicating (seemingly necessary) release. And, some days it seems hard for me to understand why people, who have not suffered from an eating disorder, or at least have never been bulimic, see it as such a far stretch. To go from eating normal, or even just being an avid dieter, to all the way over *there*—way on the other side—in some insane asylum place where you eat a pile of food only to throw it up. Many believe it requires an entire metamorphosis of your personality to make you do that to yourself. It means you are totally insane and broken.

For bulimics, it doesn't seem that way at all. It feels like a much shorter leap. Like a little hop, at most. We don't feel like we're crazy; we feel like we're in control. Like there's this secret thing we do when we're alone, and it makes us feel good and stay skinny, and it's not a big deal. Most of the time, anyway. There are other moments—when we see our distended belly in the mirror as we are shuffling to the toilet, when we are hovered over the bowl and frightened by our own involuntary, guttural wails, or, more often, when we see our vomit and snot-strewn red face in the mirror afterward—when we realize we are insane. We are broken. The moment just doesn't last long enough to take root. The black gnarly vine inside snuffs it out. All other times, what we do is just a dirty little, harmless secret. It's not a big deal.

Except that it is, because we are addicted. I'll get there. For now, let's begin the longest, most repulsive and dangerous phase of my eating disorder, shall we? My bulimia phase. *"Two fingers, not three ladies! Tssk, tssk!"*

For those who eat normal and do not have an issue with food, it's hard to imagine what would make people willingly crouch in front of the toilet and stick their fingers down their throat. Now, as I sit here writing today, knowing that I am better and I have finally healed—I have not done that in well over six months—I have to admit that it's honestly a little hard for me to imagine myself doing it now. It's hard for me to accept that I did that to myself, time and time again. Dozens, maybe even hundreds of times.

And, thankfully, after having written this whole diatribe, one of the reasons I can no longer allow myself to do that is that it would make me a royally-wretched hypocrite if I did, right? How can I possibly spout all of this "Stop now! You can do it!" stuff to you, while I'm puking every other chapter? No. I'm suffering right now, along with you. While I would love nothing more (right now!) than to go to the kitchen, make a huge pot of spaghetti, a big bowl of frosted flakes, and a pan of brownies and shove my face into a blissful food pile, I'm not. I'm sitting here, eating popcorn and writing. Because I imagine so many people out there, just like me, who know they are doing horrible things to their bodies and want nothing more than to fight that raging demon that is pushing their hand to their face, but they don't feel strong enough. I didn't either. But, here I am. Not binging. Not dipping cookies in frosting. Not ordering another patty melt at the drive-thru. Not hunched over the toilet with tears, snot, and vomit coming out of me, because I'm here, writing to you.

You, whoever reads this, have helped to keep me accountable. If I'm preaching all of this "Mind over those meandering fingers! Kick that addiction in the throat!" shit, I can't very well cave, now can I? I can't stomach (no pun, or perhaps every pun, intended) the thought of some of you, who may be finally starting to re-wire your brains back to healthy while reading this, only to find me, Chapter Thirteen, kneeled over the toilet, a slimy hand on the bowl, screaming "Don't judge me! It's okay to do *sometimes*!" Because I know it is not, in any way, okay to do it. Not even sometimes. No, for this to work, I have to believe it, too. And, I want you to know that I do. Because it has worked. And, I know exactly how hard it will be. I know how very long and tedious and scary your road ahead will be. But, you must know everything I have written here, has healed someone who suffered with an eating disorder for twenty years, someone who was bulimic for over twelve years, where some days I would go on a huge binge every single day, often twice a day, for months at a time. I did not go one day without binging during that time. Not one. And yet, these words made me who I am today—stronger, accountable, healed, and inspired to help others. But that is today. Let us venture back. To the back of my throat, to the bottom of the bowl. Imagine yourself falling down into it like Alice into the rabbit hole! You're late for a very important date!

In that moment, when you're about to do it—for the first time or the hundredth time—the absurdity of what you're about to do is the last thing on your mind. The single, solitary blazing thought in your mind is that there is food—gross, fat-causing, life-ruining food—in your stomach and it has to come out. If it doesn't come out, you will become horribly fat, within a few hours, or at least by tomorrow. It will stick on your thighs, your stomach and everyone will see you're ballooning up. You will lose control of your life. Everyone will know you are a fat, pathetic person who does not deserve to be respected, listened to, or loved. The only way to prevent that horrible outcome is to maintain the all-important "out."

It is the only thing that matters. The only thing we think about most waking hours of the day. And, my God, do I often wish I could go back in time, to so many of those moments and rip that stupid thought out of my head so I could have enjoyed myself more. I could have stopped sucking in and just laughed some more. Yes, with my stupid, huge Care Bear gut jiggling the entire time. No one would have given a fuck. We all would have just kept laughing and savored the moment. But I didn't. I sucked in. I counted in my head. And I declined that cracker with cheese on it because it would have made me fat. I didn't laugh and enjoy the moment as much because I was curled up in my head, counting, calculating, catering to my eating disorder.

I hope you're hearing the insanity of this. But it is the honest truth of what plays out in our minds. Once you've decided to go down this path and you re-wire your brain and how it processes food, "in" causes severe anxiety and then "out" is the only thing that matters. And, I have to start there, with that pressing, all-consuming thought; because it is that thought that makes you stick your fingers down your throat—for the first time and the hundredth time—because it matters way more than whatever measly impact throwing up could have on your body.

As I mentioned, for me (as I imagine it is for many), my first form of "out" was exercise. When taken to the extreme, this is already in its simplest version, a form of bulimia. Whatever calories I put in had to be (and preferably immediately) exercised out. I've already recounted for you the brutally intense (and completely unnecessary and counterproductive) exercise regimens I would put my body through during my anorexic and binge-eating phases. I would come close to fainting. I would see stars. I would piss my pants. I pushed my body harder and further than I ever did in sports, even as a gymnast. With terrible results, mind you. I was at times shockingly skinny with no fat on my body and writhing little muscles, and a poochy little gut bulging out. I hate to break it to you, but a bony rib-cage-revealing chest and flat-tire boobs are never going to pair well with thighs like a body builder. I just looked odd, unhealthy for sure, and I often got stared at when I went to the gym. So, I was working incredibly hard to refuse myself food, fight back hunger, and work out like a maniac, all to look ... sick and unapproachable. *Way to go Callie.*

And that is very hard to maintain. Your body just gets so tired. Because it's so hungry and so starved and so sick of running and squatting and lifting and pulling. This means when you do finally decide, *"Alright ten hours have passed, I think I can have a snack now,"* your body is so pissed off and starving, your hand starts going to your mouth faster and faster, your body begging it to continue, until you find you've over-eaten (which in your world means you had two extra bites, *"Heaven forbid!"*). So, now what's the only thing that has to happen? The ONLY thing that matters? You guessed it.

THE ALL-IMPORTANT OUT.

It must occur. Now. Or everything falls apart in your world. You'll get fat. You'll get ugly. Everyone will see it. You'll get depressed, be unsuccessful. These are real thoughts. Or else we wouldn't do it. If all of that "you'll get, you'll get, you'll get" is the alternative, then a little five-minute disgusting habit in the bathroom to make sure all of *that* doesn't happen, really means nothing to us. Clearly the lengths we are willing to go to, and the self-discipline it requires makes us truly capable of many, many things. Treating our body like shit is just one of our many talents!

I don't know if this is the case for most bulimics, but for me it did not start with a decision to starve, starve, starve, until it was time to eat, eat, eat then go on a wild binge followed by an expertly-performed purge. Maybe I was just slow on the uptake, but, for me, that came later, and the mental addiction it caused was truly the worst of all of it. That's the next chapter.

In the beginning, when my exhaustive anorexic and exercise-bulimic days became just too exhausting and disappointing, this forced me to go on a binge and overeat. On very bad days it was peanut butter, and I don't want to think back on the horrendous exercising I would make myself do after a peanut butter binge. On not-so-bad days it was often just easy grab-and-eat stuff around the house that, because my body was so hungry, I would over-indulge on. Cereal was a common one (I still love cereal). But I would have one bowl. Then two. Then four. And on it continued. A box of Cheezits or other hand-to-mouth salty snack was another. I would grab the box from the pantry, curl up with it on the couch, and keep eating until the entire cheesy box was gone. (One hint to those recovering: Keep less ready-to-eat, hand-to-mouth type foods in your house and more vegetables and proteins that require preparation and cooking.)

And, do know in this beginning phase, I would not eat to the point of absolute distension. That would come later. It got worse when I got better. This was just (in the grand scheme of where things were going for me) a slight overstep. I wasn't completely, miserably stuffed (I knew not yet the infinite bounds of my stretchy Wonder Stomach), this was just an accidental over-indulgence. Let's say I had eaten a whole box of Cheezits. And remember, I was an anorexic-exercise-bulimic so I probably hadn't eaten anything substantial in at least six or seven hours before this, if not longer. That means very little going in. And, I probably worked out at least once, if not twice that day already; or, trust me, I wouldn't have even let myself indulge *any* crackers at all. So, let's just guess that somewhere around 400 calories had already gone out, not including the calories burned just from walking, talking, sitting, thinking, etc., *i.e.*, the normal calories you burn in a regular, no exercise day. Whatever my 'out' amount was, I was high on the negative side of the scale and in need of calories going in. Cheezits have around 150 calories per serving and around twelve servings per box.

Meaning, even if I had indulged in an entire box and that's all I had for the day, that's only 1,800 calories. I was still totally fine and could still stand to eat a small healthy meal that day *and still be in a totally-acceptable range*. Without working out at all!

Now, is a box of Cheezits a healthy meal? No. But, is it one I need to purge from my body with another hour of exercise or by throwing up?

NO.

But Callie didn't think like that. She indulged. She was bad. *"Shame on you, Callie!"* *whack!* goes the whip. Her body needed to be punished. And I would then attempt to either work it off or throw it up. I experimented very briefly with laxatives and weightloss pills, Metabolife primarily, with terrible, frightening results. You'll see in the "things I do not want to confess" section. (Look forward to that one, trust me. Know that the current man in my life has forgiven me for the part of my ass that occasionally falls out that I have to stuff back in. Good times.) No, the laxative phase, thankfully, did not last long. But, the bulimia phase didn't really take off after the first few times I tried to throw up what I had just eaten. Mostly because I wasn't very good at it. It's not like anyone puts a manual out there on how to be a good bulimic—*i.e.*, explaining what foods are easier to purge, what the best technique is for causing involuntary gut-wrenching, etc. *Best Practices of Bulimics* is never going to be up there with Emily Post's book on Etiquette (not publicly at least). So, everything I tried was in complete, isolated experimentation.

As is the case with most people who have an eating disorder, often there is not a single person in their life who knows about it. Or at least who they have told about it. I hate to tell you this, Disorderlies, but if you are fostering a severe eating disorder and think the people in your life who love you and see you every day do not know, *you're wrong*. They can see, hear, smell, or even just sense it. If they haven't yet said anything, they're just too afraid to confront you about it, fearing it will make you shut them out and perhaps get worse. (And you know that is probably exactly what will happen.) So, I would imagine anyone who becomes a functional but habitual bulimic is self-taught. It's rare that anyone kneels down with us by the toilet and teaches us how to do this.

For this reason, I was, initially, not very good at it. I know now that is because I was not eating the kinds of foods that are easier to throw up than others. I was not pressing on the right part of my throat. And I hate that I know these things now. I wish I had remained bad at it and quit. But, I didn't. *"Daddy never raised a quitter!"* I warned you, we're stubborn. People with eating disorders are very strong-willed and self-disciplined. Know that. Thankfully, the fact that I was not very good at it at the time, coupled with a number of other factors in my life—I was married and lived with someone and was on a tight budget (so I couldn't afford to buy enormous amounts of expensive binge food)—meant that I did not take to bulimia quickly. It was just the occasional, mostly-unsuccessful attempt to purge food when I felt I had gone too far and didn't have any other option. It would be several more years, finishing out law school and starting my practice, of continued anorexic-exercise-bulimia with the occasional attempt to throw my food up, before full-blown bulimia took hold.

At this point on my timeline, I was twenty-six. I was a lawyer, a pretty impressive sole-female litigator, actually, at a defense firm with a very bright and promising future there. I made over six figures. I was three years married to a pretty decent guy. (I mean, they're all somewhat of a compromise, right?) I owned my own house (well, the mortgage, at least, but I was easily able to pay it). Why on earth would a person like me even: a) continue my struggle with food and the punishment it forced me to inflict on my body or, better yet; b) decide to make it all so much worse by becoming a full-blown, everyday bulimic? I am truly trying to answer this question both for myself and for any of you who wonder why you or a loved one went down this road.

I know I was stressed to the max. However hard I thought law school was and studying for the Bar, the practice was way harder, far more intimidating and frightening. My job caused me many nightmares, even daymares (if that's a word). With the enormous (mostly self-inflicted, but this is a trait of Type A people that will likely never be changed) pressure and expectation I forced on myself, I felt like I didn't have time to prepare and cook healthy foods. Plus, I didn't know how to cook and didn't believe I had the time to learn. At the center of it all, I was super stressed, beyond busy with way too many obligations to maintain (and *also* maintain an eating disorder) and I had a bigger problem. I now needed to look and feel skinny to keep my job. Sound crazy? It's really not. This skinny-equals-successful regime does not apply only to fashion models, gymnasts, recording artists, etc. It applies to anyone whose self-confidence derives from how they feel about their appearance. How many people do you think that is?

*I hope you said, "just about everyone," because that feels about right.*

I know this may sound a little strange (that bulimia enabled me to maintain my successful career), but it was one of my biggest influencing factors. As often the only female in a room full of sharp, confident male lawyers, if I felt fat that day, I felt like they could see it and wouldn't take me as seriously. *"She's just a sad, fat girl who doesn't have anything smart to contribute."* If you're going to be a top-performing female litigator in a largely-male world, doing it while turning heads and looking svelte in a tiny pencil skirt and five-inch heels (because it makes me feel and act confident) is exceedingly more effective. When I felt fat, my confidence suffered and so did my performance, which in that cut-throat environment needed, every day, every hour, every minute, to be exceptional. Suddenly that fear I'd had all along—that if I got fat, everyone would see and would not take me seriously and I would not be successful—was <u>a reality</u>.

Have you ever felt this way? That looking, or even just *feeling*, fat would translate to immediate career failure?

It did for me. Because my *perception* of how I looked had a direct impact on how well I actually *performed* my job, I literally *had* to stay skinny to keep excelling at my job. And, I didn't have the time (I believed) to do it any other way. Stuff always has to go in, or you'll faint at your desk and that would be embarrassing. Even with an eating disorder, we know we have to occasionally eat so we can still stand upright and walk and talk. You know ... that silly stuff. But for us, bulimics, we would like most of it to go out, so that when we stand upright and walk and talk and do all of that important stuff, *we're skinny*. We're also often busy and successful, with very high-stress jobs and very little time to spare.

A word on successful people and eating disorders:

I honestly think some of the most egregious bulimics out there are probably also some of the most high-paid, exceedingly hard-working and highly-successful people. (Think intense high-stakes litigators, renowned cardiac surgeons, six-figure stock traders, international negotiators, CEOs and directors at million-dollar companies.) This is because the disorder feeds off a stomach-clenching desire to inflict control, to have the tenacity and durability to push something so hard, either hunger down or food back up, until you have conquered it. Many bulimics probably see their pattern as one of success. They desire and crave food, yet food is the very antithesis of what they desire and crave even more (that is to feel powerful and skinny), so they see their disorder as not the problem but the solution. *"I have found a way to eat as much as I want and be as skinny as I want. I win. Take that food."*

I'm sure this is an honest thought for many thriving, successful bulimics. Our rationale is so screwed up. Any excuse we can come up with to make it—the process of stuffing our body with absurd portions of unhealthy food, then violently and disgustingly heaving it back up—a necessary, warranted, or even *good* thing for our body, we will pounce on it. Perhaps you've heard or told yourself some of these: *"It's my release; it helps ease my stress. I need it to be able to hunker down and do four more hours of work tonight. I need it to feel powerful in the courtroom. I need it to feel powerful in the operating room. I need it to feel powerful in the board room. I need it to feel powerful in the <u>insert your profession here</u> room. Many cancer patients have probably puked way more than me and they're fine. My teeth all look great; no part of my body is telling me this is harming me in any way. I deserve it; I worked my ass off today and closed that deal. Saved that child. Won that case. Finally stood up to that douchebag."* Whatever it may be, we'll justify it. A purge is totally deserved, earned and necessary—healthy even. Exceedingly minor compared to the super-stressful shit we handle every day with a quick wit and tiny waist. *There's no sick person with a repulsive, dangerous addiction here. Noooooo … Just a professional badass with a little secret. Shhh!*

On some of this I can only surmise because, for the very scenario I stated above (*"Shhh, it's a secret"*), it's tough to get accurate statistics on bulimics. We're not just going to disclose that shit. *Are you crazy?! Why do you think we go to such lengths to hide it?* So, it would be hard to say "90% of all bulimics are functioning, successful adults," because most bulimics would never divulge their sinful little secret. But, I'll bet if you're reading this and you've been bulimic for some time, it's highly likely you're a high-performing, fast-paced adult who can handle stress well and likely has a lot of responsibility—corporate, domestic, dangerous, lucrative, or otherwise. Part of the reason you got to that point is probably because you're incredibly hard on yourself. It's also the reason you're bulimic.

For many, it is this type of lifestyle that fosters an eating disorder; because it is hard to maintain good health when your job is super stressful, consumes you, and doesn't leave much time outside to focus on grocery shopping, cooking healthy meals and exercising every day. If you are, like I was—usually confined to an office setting all day and therefore mostly inactive, albeit very stressed with your mental gears smoking and threatening to spin off their spokes—by the time you get home, the only thing you want to do is throw on sweats, plop on the couch, and watch mindless TV to make your mental soundtrack finally stop. *Shut that thing down, she's smoking anyway.* But you also want to (have to, dammit!) eat. And, when your ability to perform your job well is literally tied directly to your internal perception of how you look that day, eating becomes a problem. Meaning, if the time you think must be devoted to a healthy lifestyle doesn't jibe with your work-then-veg routine *and* you enjoy the pleasure of binging, the choice is really rather simple.

Another fact I'll just go out on a limb and surmise is true: Most bulimics live alone.

It's just easier. And because I catered my career and my disease more than anything else in my life then, I would soon live alone, too. That's coming.

But, at the time, I felt I had found a solution. There I was. A young, hard-working attorney. Not just wanting, but *needing* to look and feel skinny and an option presented itself to me that took (in my mind) little time and effort—just a five-minute maneuver that effectively accomplished a very necessary task. The choice was then, frankly, very easy to make. I didn't have time to cook healthy food. I didn't have time to work out. And I damn sure didn't have time to admit I had a disorder and put my busy, stressful, important job on hold while I tried to rehab myself. Yet, I still had to occasionally eat so I could do said busy, stressful, important job. So, the decision was already made. *"Puke and go lady. They need you at the office."*

Man, that all sounds so backwards and convoluted now. But, I did it. I chose that path for years. And I'm a smart, intelligent person. So, I had to literally try to go back in time and ask myself the important question. I imagine my current self, sitting on the couch, next to the old Callie, who is hunched over two big Tupperware containers; one filled with cupcakes, frosting, ice cream and the other with McDonald's fries smothered in cheese sauce, shoveling in heaping spoonfuls. Smears of frosting and cheese graze her cheeks as I hold a microphone out and ask her: "Why are you doing this?" And when I do, that seems to be the answer Back-Then Bulimic Callie would have given me. "I'm busy. I don't have time. I can't eat normal because I have a retarded body, so there's no other way. Now get out of my way to the toilet. This interview is over."

I can see, now, this was the mindset that started it. And once this seed was planted—that throwing up my food was the quickest and most effective option to accomplish my necessary *out*—I knew then I just needed to make the option easier as well. *"You just need to get better at it, Callie."*

Boy, did I ... We are all incredibly-stubborn over-achievers, aren't we?

It all got so much worse when I got better.

# CHAPTER NINE

# IT GOT BAD WHEN I GOT BETTER: CUE MY BULIMIA BUDDY

Not got better, got healthy. *Pssshhh! No. Are you crazy?* I was way too far gone at that point. I got better at *it*: binging and purging. And, yes, you can get better at binging. It takes a very disciplined and trained stomach to put down two burgers and a large pizza (I'm not exaggerating) and store them until you're ready to eject them, then shrink right back down for another round. That's one talented stomach right there. And one seriously-broken adult.

Imagine me in a dating game: *"Hi my name is Callie. I'm a lawyer. I'm blonde, skinny, and funny. Oh, oh, and I can eat a whole*

*pizza and throw it right back up. Every bite. In thirty minutes.
Wanna see?"*

Man, she's a winner. What do we have for her, Johnny?

A hernia, almost. I don't want to know how close I came ...

But, how does one progress down this road? Improve their
binge-and-purge process? At the time, I was not throwing up
every day. Rather, I was still skipping breakfast, sticking to salads
mostly at my desk for lunch, and messing around with stupid
diet food (packaged crap that promises low calories, low fat,
but is not actual food). Dinner was always the worst, because
you're supposed to go home and cook a nice meal and enjoy it
with your family, right? *Please! Ain't nobody got time for that.*

Not in my fast-paced busy lawyer days, anyway. I usually worked
until the cleaning lady came to our office, close to 7:00 p.m. (I
told myself this is what the young, driven associate is supposed
to do: be the first one there and the last to leave.) This was all
self-inflicted. My partners, while aggressive and equally busy
themselves, often encouraged me to leave earlier and take
more time off. *"Time off is for pussies!"* Isn't this the crap we
Type A'ers say internally? We are so hard on ourselves.

But, this put me home around 7:30 p.m. every evening, in no
mood to cook a dinner, so Husband and I usually heated up
something or got carryout. And while I tried to eat somewhat
healthy meals and somewhat small portions, the frequent
super stressful day would sometimes set me off and I would eat
two or three extra helpings. I knew the minute I started to do
this, the minute I got two bites past what was acceptable, I was
going to have to throw it up. To me, there was no other choice.

I was too tired to work out then and it was already *down*. So, there was only one way to get it back up. But then, there was the pesky husband to deal with.

*"Why is he always arooouuund?"* I seriously remember asking myself this. Like he didn't live there. Like he wasn't supposed to want to spend his evenings with me. But, you can imagine during this time how stressed I was. How most of the time I was frustrated, irritated, and *hungry* which made me not the nicest person to be around. At home anyway, when I finally took my put-together, in-control lawyer mask off. And, who do you always take your raw emotions out on? The people that are closest to you. I'll be the first to admit I was a pretty snarly bitch to my husband at times. Now, was he in many ways a deadbeat who couldn't earn a buck and lazily relied on me to be the breadwinner and carry the both of us? You bet. But, that still doesn't justify the way I treated him at times.

If you read this: *Sorry Husband.*

But, when you work a very hard, stressful day at the office and the last thing you want to do is go home and fight with your spouse, what do you do? Quiz Time!

You got it. Head straight to the bar. I found it much easier to go there and unwind over a few drinks than endure the tense, prickly place home had become. Plus, no one expected you to eat dinner at the bar *and* alcohol is a great appetite suppressant. It was a win-win. We won't talk about my escalated drinking and many intoxicated drives home. That's another book, and another evil confronted and conquered in the life and times of Callie. But it was in a dark corner of a loud bar that the worst thing that could possibly happen to someone with an eating disorder happened to me.

"I am totally going through Sonic on the way home," she said, which seemed odd, because I'd never seen her eat. Granted, I had only known her for a few weeks when I started going to this particular dive bar after work because many other lawyers went there, she being one. But we clicked instantly, grew surprisingly close instantly. She, too, was a lawyer. Her days were stressful, too. Money, for her, was also good, but the only thing we had time to spend it on were booze and bills. And, much like me, she was funny, witty, also a pretty badass female lawyer in her own male-dominated sector. Ironically, she was also pretty, blonde, and skinny, too.

"I just ... uggh ... it's been a day," she said, which instantly told me food was, like me, not sustenance for her. Rather, it was a tool. However, of all the things she and I had talked about at length— men, work, family, booze, sex, old boyfriends even—food was not something that had ever come up. My silence peaked her curiosity. Being a far more experienced bulimic than me, I'm sure she sensed it about me sooner than I did her. She gave me a probing look, waiting for me to respond. Nothing came.

"It just. It helps me ... check out at the end of the day. Unwind and start again." Her eyes were now searing mine, which dropped instantly down to my drink. "You know?" she asked tentatively, which was a clever way to get the answer she was looking for. Then I knew. It hit me like a lead weight on my shoulders.

*She's bulimic, too.*

I hesitated for a long time before answering. This was my one big, dark secret. The dirty little thing I did on occasion that no one needed to know about. *That no one in the whole world knew about.* And, here I was about to let it out. Flash it for someone to see, someone I hadn't really known that long. But, here she was, the first person I had met who was like me in this one very difficult-to-understand way, and she was just … at ease with it. It was acceptable and okay. It was almost thrilling. I had found her.

My Bulimia Buddy!

After I nodded in response to her question that night and we both let sly smiles spread across our faces, it became a shameful, gross thing no longer. Everything changed. Now it was a devilish, fun little secret we shared. Now I had a friend who did it, too. Now it wasn't so weird and incomprehensible. It wasn't such a *bad* thing to do.

Except that it is, and always will be. Whether you do it alone. Or with a friend. Or in a whole group circle, holding each other's hair back and taking turns. It will always be disgusting. But, only Healed Callie knows that now. Bulimic Callie, who had just found a friend in her sickness, didn't think that at all. Meeting someone else who did it, too—who condoned it, too—was the worst thing that could have ever happened to me. Because with Charlene as my new bulimia sponsor, I got better at it.

It was weird that we never had another face-to-face conversation about it, until the last night I ever saw Charlene. The bloody end. But we "talked" about it often, in code. Toward the end of a rough work day, both of us often working till close to eight, and I would text her to see if she wanted to grab a few drinks. If she wasn't up for drinks, her response would often be:

"At Sonic." Which definitely answered my question (no drinks tonight) and easily inspired the same thought I was having about how to spend the evening.

"You?" she'd ask.

"McDonald's here I come," I would reply.

On other days:

"What a fucking day at the office, huh? I hate this job. Pizza Hut, you?" she'd text with a winkey face.

"Whataburger," I would respond with a little fist bump. I wonder if they'll come up with a stuffing-your-face or throwing-up emoji so us bulimics can have fun texting with little happy icons, too.

The problem with this was that it became fun! Yes, fun. Like a new hobby. The fact that Charlene and I were both doing it. Both of us successful, pretty, accomplished women and we were both stuffing our face at the drive-thru. Hurling up our guts up every night wasn't weird or bad, because we were *both* doing it. It was suddenly okay. Something I actually even looked forward to because it was such a release. And, with Charlene on board I learned a few tricks of the trade. Like fast food.

"Fast in, fast out," I remember her texting one time. And she was so right! While I had learned ATJ (at the John) that soft, moist foods were easier to get back up than dry, thick ones— like peanut butter, do NOT try to throw that up at home—I had been relying on cereal, ice cream, pastas swimming in Alfredo, fries dipped in Alfredo, pizza, also dipped in Alfredo. I love Alfredo. Now, Alfredo sat as a sad, second-rate contender, once I discovered the ultimate bulimic lube. Grease! My God that stuff's good. Everything goes so easily down and comes so easily back up! And tastes so damn good, too. In all my years before Charlene, I hadn't yet thought about fast food. Probably because I hadn't been creative enough to think I could gorge in the sanctity of my car and throw up at any restaurant or business with a single locked stall.

Yes, I did this in my business suit on occasion. No, I don't want to remember what it looked like.

You could also so easily throw the evidence away, and it was like it literally never happened. I came home content, skinny, my tension and stress happily released, at least momentarily. Even with a friend just a few clicks away who shared the same simple pleasure, too. I was literally happy about this situation. And, that proved to be a big problem for my husband. Spoiler alert! The hubby and I did not last. When your most important thing is work, your favorite person to unwind with is not your spouse, your favorite place is not home, and your favorite thing to do you cannot do with him around, the husband starts to become a huge irritant in your life, an annoying thing that's always around and hindering your pleasure. Wouldn't want the pesky husband frowning and tssk-tssk'ing me while I ate a whole stuffed crust pizza dipped in cheese. *"That's no fun. Sorry hubby, but you gotta go."*

Yes, I know how awful this sounds. But I believe if many bulimics are honest with themselves, they have probably felt this way about many important people in their lives when they were—or unfortunately may *be* right now—deep in the grip of that vicious disease. While I do feel badly for so frequently shunning him, I also know now we made the wrong decision marrying so early; because we hadn't yet grown into the adults we were going to be and we were in no way right for each other, barely even compatible as the years passed. Our divorce was inevitable, regardless of my eating disorder, but I'm sure it brought it on much sooner because it is such a solitary sickness. It is something you have to push people out of your life to protect. Because we do want to protect it. More than most anything else in our lives.

What I feel worse about is the torture I inflicted on my body for those many, many years. Because once the divorce was inevitable, I then moved out and into my own apartment and found myself living alone for the first time since college, since all of this began. And, if there is any type of person who should not live alone, it is someone suffering from bulimia. With the ability to indulge our craving anytime we want, without having to hide it, we completely embrace it. No more locked bathroom doors. No more hiding it away. No more quick, frantic clean-up of the mess. No more worrying about multiple flushes or puking sounds. *"Smell? What smell?"* No one's there. No one cares! You can even pick back up with that half-eaten ice cream cake if you'd like and start right back in after purging. It's likely still sitting on the coffee table taunting you anyway.

It's bad. Living alone is the worst thing you, as a bulimic, can do. If you are seriously trying to quit this disgusting habit and you currently live alone, find a roommate! And fast! It is one of the best ways to start holding yourself accountable. And, who knows, you just might have more fun sharing a healthy meal or snack with a friend than binging alone. Just maybe.

And if you, too, find a Bulimia Buddy—someone who does it, too, and who makes you think it's really not a harmful, dangerous, disgusting (gross!) thing to do—do not move in together!

You thought I was going to say unfriend said Buddy, didn't you? Perhaps that's necessary. Or perhaps you two can stop together and heal together and it will be easier because you have support. *I doubt it.* You'll probably just start bringing one another down. But if not, and you find that person only encourages you to do it more then, yes, some unfriending is definitely in order.

This was the heyday of my bulimia phase. I learned the beautiful passage, in and out, of greasy fast food. As a high-paid, high-stakes lawyer, I had plenty of money to spend on my greasy food. Newly-divorced, I lived alone, which meant I now had plenty of time at home to spend with my greasy food. My disgusting routine was completely hidden in the security and solitude of my apartment. Without having to do any cooking, grocery shopping, yardwork, big house cleaning, or spending time with a loved one once I got home—*Who wants to do that?*—I had plenty of time to spend embracing my disease, binging and purging back-to-back some evenings. I also had the time and solace to work out like a maniac again, often twice a day, often to the point of fainting. *"Hell yeah! There goes that thigh fat!"*

Newly-divorced also meant I had emphatic new motivation to get back to skinny so I could traipse around like a vixen in my sexy work heels and attract someone new! The thought of actually bringing a new man into my life and sharing it, and my living space, with him never crossed my mind. *"Are you kidding? And give up my pimp purge pad? Please!"* I just wanted to bang the occasional hot dude. And I definitely wanted to look hot and skinny when I did. No more fat, married Callie, all squishy in her pantyhose.

*And I had a friend.* Who shared my dark secret, so everything was totally fine. Charlene and I both lived alone. We could both curl up on our respective couches with four bins of greasy, fatty, heavenly cheesy foods around us, often in big over-sized Tupperware tubs (because you didn't want your binge session to be frequently interrupted by having to refill) and a gallon of chocolate milk on the end table, drank straight from the jug, then *binge* without judgment. Without needing to hide or cover it up immediately. We could leave our gross, greasy piles on the coffee table in the living room while we shuffled, hunched-over to the toilet to do our business, which was now easier, because I was eating super easily puke-upable foods (that was a word then). The only problem with that was, when you came back from the bathroom, feeling decadently skinny, you would often look at the half-eaten food strewn everywhere and think about doing it again.

Yes. Again. Right then. I know many bulimics who have confessed to binging again, immediately after a purge. The craving is insurmountable. But you tell yourself it's fine. *"Charlene does it and I'm sure hundreds of others do, too. No one's getting seriously hurt from it."*

*But then someone did.* Charlene. An event that sent her to the hospital as a direct result of her throwing up.

This did not stop me. This phase, when I was living alone, because of the freedom and privacy it afforded me, molded the worst part of this disease for me. The hardest thing to overcome. The reason I continued doing these horrible things to my body—long after I realized how dangerous and potentially deadly they were, and long after they had cost me friends and relationships, money and time, and long after I realized they do not work.

Half of the crap I'm spouting in this book you probably already know. Of course stuffing your stomach to the point of distension then heaving it all up in a thunderous, violent roar through your throat is not good for you and is not the best way to look and feel the way you want to. You know all of this and so did I. But it did not stop me.

Because I had become addicted.

Food was no longer my enemy. It was my very dangerous drug.

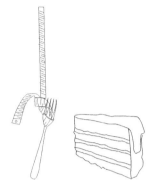

**CHAPTER TEN**

# IT GOT WORSE WHEN I GOT ADDICTED: MY DRIVE-THRU PHASE

It would start to creep into my thoughts in the afternoon at the office. Its soothing fingers crawling up my neck and wrapping around my brain. *Food.* It was an intoxicating endorphin rush. Having spent all day refusing myself any filling or indulgent food, now the dam was about to burst. I got high thinking about all the delicious foods I was about to eat. Fries dipped in cheese sauce. Warm cake and frosting piled covered with ice cream. An entire pack of Oreos dunked in milk. No wait, poured in a bowl of milk! Oreo cereal! Three greasy cheeseburgers, each with two extra slices of cheese. Taco Bell burritos, each bite dipped in cheese. A stuffed crust cheese pizza, each bite dipped in cheese.

Obviously, my drug of choice is cheese.

And I truly consider it a drug because nothing in my life provided me the same "high" that food could. What had previously just been something I did a couple of times a week—while saddled with work, the husband, house chores, and little time to work out—to get at least some of my input "out," had now (post-divorce, in my solitary apartment) morphed into something completely different. Food could either be taken in tiny anorexic-level portions (my 600-calories-a-day routine) or I could succumb to an indulgent, deeply-satisfying binge. One of two choices. As if on a Food Scale I was allowed only up to 10% or I had to go the full 100% then puke my guts out. And, to be more accurate, it was like 125% because any bulimic will tell you: the fuller you get, the more easily your body ejects it out. We eat past the point of pleasure, to the point of pain and misery, because it's necessary for performance. It's disgusting that I know these truths. But, there were only two choices I allowed myself (Extreme Option A or Even-More-Extreme Option B) and, in doing so, I created a devastatingly-addictive reward for enduring hunger. I now had a drug I began to crave and consume every day.

Even now, months and months healed, my mind can still drift back to the piles of grease and cheese I was allowed to indulge and the craving is still there. Those tingly fingers still climb my neck and ignite my saliva glands as they crawl under my scalp to my brain. It's just that my mind is now healthier and strong enough to tamp the feeling down. When it starts to build, I make myself walk to a toilet (wherever I'm at) and try to imagine myself hunched over it, puking violently—my red neck inflamed and bulging with the thunderous chunks that are coming up. Then I see my face, as it always was when I finished, with smears of vomit around my mouth, two streams of snot down to my lips and black smudges under my eyes. The tears that would come involuntarily—my body's physical pleas, begging me to stop.

It's not pretty. And it's an image that reminds me I now have more respect for my body than that. I now know whatever irritation, anger, fear, frustration, or even just boredom I am feeling in that moment that is letting me allow that craving to grow, will not be cured by doing that. However yucky and fat I am feeling that day, I will not feel any better after doing *that*. I will probably feel worse because then, in addition to feeling yucky and fat, I will also feel disappointed in myself, embarrassed and angry at my own failure and my own horrid treatment of my own body. Rather, the pride I now take in overcoming that weak desire by eating a healthy snack, going for a walk, reading (or perhaps even writing!) a chapter in a good book is far more rewarding than doing *that*. I can feel my body thanking me and I get excited to reward her with a healthy, filling meal later that evening. Now, when the craving strikes, I often drive straight to the grocery store, look up a delicious, healthy recipe in the magazine section and then shop around for the ingredients I'll need to make it that night and the craving weakens. I know I have put a healthier, far more fulfilling reward on the horizon and I look forward to that more. Any day you can refrain from voluntarily throwing up is a good day. It is one more toward a healthier, far more fulfilling life.

But that is the current Me speaking. Happy, Healthy Callie. The laughable, pathetic version of myself, who in those days spent at least five out of six nights shoveling food in until my stomach was so sick and swollen I could not stand upright, shuffling my distended tummy to the bathroom, only to wrench the entirety

of stomach contents out and perhaps start eating again right
afterward, is a reality I have to face. I was that person. I did
those things. For years. Because nothing in my life brought me
the kind of ecstatic satisfaction that binge-eating did. Nothing.
Isn't that so stupid and sad?

"Callie, would you like go horse-back riding on the beach?"
"No thanks, I just put in an order for a cheese pizza."

"Callie, would you like to go to a dance studio and learn a new
jazz-funk routine with me?
"Sorry, I've got a date with a bowl, a spoon, and my couch."

"Callie, I've got a few super-hot, horny guys over here. Want to
come have the most memorable sex of our lives?"
"Tempting, but nah. I'd rather eat waffles instead."

Okay that last one might have swayed me. But it was rare that
there was literally anything I liked to do *more* than binging.
Nothing else gave me quite the orgasmic high. There were
only a few other things I did in my life. Work, because I had to.
Work out, because I had to (stay skinny and pretty). Or drink
with friends and flirt with men. The former because it took my
mind off of food. The latter because random sex post-divorce
was sometimes fun. More often a disappointing headache, but
occasionally fun. But none of these things encroached on my
main hobby. My addiction. I would not allow them.

It pains me to think how many hours I spent doing that, which
translates to days, which may very well translate to months. I'm
not kidding. Hell, this book is about finally opening all of this
nasty shit up and getting it out, once and for all, so let's just
go there. I was daily bulimic for roughly five years, binging and

purging anywhere from four to seven times a week. We'll say roughly 70% of those days being binge days, with each session lasting about an hour. Cue the Schoolhouse Rock music. Let's do this!

5 years x 365 days = 1,825 days
70% of 1,825 = 1,277 days
1,277 days x 1 hour/day = 1,277 hours
1,277 hours divided by 24 = 53 days.

Fifty-fucking three. Where I spend each hour of *each* day eating to the point of distension then puking, eating then puking, eating then puking. I really feel like the armless Sisyphus now. Imagine if someone told you today that starting tomorrow morning, you're not going to the office. You're not going to work. You're not even going to get dressed or leave your home. You're going to sit on the couch in your PJs and stuff your face till your stomach hurts. Then you're going to kneel before the toilet and stick your finger down your throat until everything comes back up. Everything. All of it. Then you're going to come back to the couch and start over again. Twenty-four hours a day until fifty-three days have passed.

And I have to laugh if you're telling yourself, *"Oh that's just silly, no one can do it twenty-four hours every day, non-stop without sleeping."*

And I would say, "You're right! You want to sleep at night, and then start back every morning? Okay, that's fine. You just now have to do it for 106 days. Sound good?"

And, there you have it. At that rate, I spent over three months of my life eating and puking every hour from sun up until bedtime. Imagine if someone told you that you had to start that regimen tomorrow. Would you sign up? Fuck no! Obviously not. But, that's the seductive nature of the disease. It's accepted, welcomed, and eventually accommodated in small, yet increasing doses. And if it's just once a day, or a couple of times a week, it's not really that *bad* of a thing, right? If you want to continue indulging your addiction and thinking that way, that's on you. But there is no denying there is truly only one thing that really matters in this life. The one and only thing that cannot be replaced or retrieved once it is gone is time. Moments that cannot be relived. Experiences and connections you missed because you chose instead to be alone and do *that*.

I see that now. I did not see it then.

Three more cataclysmic events had to occur before I would finally (*finally!*) decide to stop. And the decision is just step one. The follow-through is a whole infuriating other.

This was well into my living-alone, doing-it-every-day (if not twice) phase. I had dropped the extra weight of the husband and another twenty to boot with the time and freedom to binge on both exercising and purging. I don't need to recount in great detail the routine of my sad life then. I would go to the office around 6:00 a.m., the morning fueled on coffee alone. Lunch would usually be spent at my desk with a light salad and Diet Coke (or out with friends ... with a light salad and Diet Coke) until my cravings started to take over—whispers too loud to ignore. If I could not leave the office "early" (which meant between 4:30 and 5:00 p.m. with the rest of the normal attorneys), I would indulge myself an extra cup of piping hot coffee or a diet soda to get myself through the afternoon.

Then, when all of my work (that I wanted to accomplish that day at least) was finally done to my satisfaction and I was willing to allow myself to shut down, my endorphin rush would begin. That tantalizing flow of juice through my veins that told me I was about to give in. I was about to let myself fall into that blissful abyss. That vat of warm honey, the comfort and satisfaction of my drug.

It was intoxicating. It was mind-altering. A blissful release. This is what makes it so hard to quit. One deliciously-satisfying hour followed by a few unsanitary minutes in the bathroom and then *voila* it never happened. *"I didn't just do that. Nope, not me. Skinny and pretty me."*

If I could go back in time, I would punch myself. I really would. I would love to. If anyone out there gets wind of a time travel machine that's somewhat reliable, please let me know. I was such an idiot. A wasteful, dangerous, selfish, moronic idiot. But we're just addicted, that's all. To a drug that's dangerous, disgusting, and deadly. I guess looking at it that way, does it change your opinion of you at all? You are no better than a heroin addict. How little do you think of those people, lying on the streets in their dirty, disheveled clothes with cracked teeth and grimy hair? You think they're weak, don't you? Super strong and confident You? Skinny and smart You?

They're just addicted, same as you. They're just not hiding it, like you.

My eating disorder was its absolute worst when I was addicted. My craving for a binge overtook friends, family, invitations, sometimes even work obligations. It was the thing I wanted to do the most. The only thing that could relieve the surge of stress, irritation, worry, and anger that seemed to build every day in my frazzled legal mind. And the one thing I was willing to go to incredible, disgusting lengths to protect and continue. Before I share the three pinnacle events that finally culminated into my decision to stop, it's probably best I go ahead and share these. The things I sometimes cannot believe I did. And know that no matter how revolting, embarrassing, and dangerous you find these things are, they did not stop me.

Hopefully, they alone can help stop some of you. It's time to confess.

**CHAPTER ELEVEN**

# THE THINGS I DO NOT WANT TO (BUT MUST) CONFESS

I really don't want to have to put these things down on paper. These are the things I hope I can convince my current Guy—my lover, my partner, my best friend—that he does not need to know about me and keep his eyes away. These are things I fear will forever change people's perception of me and decide I am not the kind of respectable, smart, clean person they thought I was. That they will no longer want to continue to employ me, work with me, talk to me, love me, even look at me.

These are the things I do not want to confess.

But, I also know I began writing this book for a reason. Because if you're ever going to get better, finally decide to stop and focus on healing, you just have to put it out there. You cannot lie about it. You can no longer hide it. You have to find someone in your life that you trust will face it with you, help and support you, and see you through it. These are the kinds of people you need to surround yourself with anyway, because they won't think any less of you for having an eating disorder. They will think more of you for overcoming it. Whether you like it or not, whether you're proud of it or not, you chose to go down this road. You chose to do these horrendous things to yourself, likely for years. You chose to make this a part of your history, which makes it a part of *you*, part of who you are. That is why I have to get these things out.

I must confess.

That is why I started writing this book. And this book is half the reason I am now healed. Many, many (many!) times when I wanted to plunge down that slick path to pleasure, I wanted to jump in my car and head to the drive-thru to stuff my face full of doughnuts and burritos. I wanted that endorphin high of a completely concave, empty stomach right after throwing up. But instead, I would come back here. To this keyboard. To this white screen with the black letters. To continue putting down stories, moments, and memories of times that I am not proud of to remind me why I finally chose to quit. Often, the writing of this book prevented me from slipping. It was a huge part of my recovery path. You may want to start writing your own journal, too. I found documenting my mental and physical journey through all of this to be frightening, embarrassing, insightful but overall therapeutic. But, if you start writing, you have to promise yourself it's because you are going to someday show it to someone. You are going to share your story with someone you trust who loves you, so you can finally start to heal.

And it means you have to re-live your worst moments. The most sickening ones. The most petrifying, mortifying ones.

Which is why I must now share here. I need to go all the way. To tell you some of the things I've been holding back because they are most repulsive. They are things I wish most people will never know about me. But I share them here, with whoever picks this book up looking for help, in hopes that these horrendous confessions might give you the strength you need to finally stop. I hope experiences like these can be the realization that finally slaps you in the face, holds a mirror up to your own eating disorder, and helps you see the reality of what you are doing to yourself.

I'm not going to go into a ton of detail here, because it's not necessary. The fact that these things happened—or, rather, that I did these horribly stupid and dangerous things to myself, yet they did not stop me—is enough.

Okay, here goes. Breathe in. Breathe out, Callie.

- I once threw up until my nose bled. It was the first and only time I tried to throw up peanut butter. I was infuriated with my defiant body for keeping it down, refusing me the relief of getting it back up. It was the last time I binged on peanut butter, but not the last time I would heave until my nose bled. This did not stop me.

- I once slapped my friend in a restaurant for trying to help me box the remainder of a salad (of which I had eaten three measly bites and spent the rest of the hour pushing it around on my plate), because she made a comment about how little I had eaten. A few more episodes like this and one last nasty confrontation where I sided with my eating disorder and we didn't remain friends much longer.

- Another friend threw my bottle of Metabolife pills at me at a bar and told me I was "Sick!" Embarrassed beyond belief, I still dropped to my knees and picked up all the dirty pills from the gross, sticky bar floor. We, too, did not remain friends much longer.

- I once had to pull off the side of the interstate, almost not making it in time to open my car door and puke into the grass. My heart started beating wildly, my hands sweating so much they were slipping off the wheel, before my mouth instantly filled with saliva and I knew I was going to throw up. I had taken four Metabolife pills right after an intense workout, my second of the day (both the workout and pill dose).

- After several not-so-friendly comments from friends and family about my yellow butter-spray hands, I went to see a nutritionist at the University, because I wanted to ask her, while hiding my hands, if it was possible to eat too much beta carotene. "Perhaps," she said. "Depending on the amount," while she eyed me curiously, easily and accurately suspecting a rampant eating disorder, and asked if I wanted to make another appointment. I declined and never went back. My body mass index ("BMI") which she measured and charted that day was 19.2, which, for me, I can assure you, is much too gaunt.

-   I mentioned the yellow fingers, right? I seriously ate something, not meant to be eaten in huge quantities, not even good in those quantities, and embarrassingly-weird in those quantities, until my fingers turned yellow, which I can assure you is equally embarrassing and weird. This did not stop me.

-   I once found myself curled up in a ball on my bedroom floor (I was married at the time and had locked the door to our bedroom in case my husband came back inside). I was sweating profusely, my heart beating violently against my ribcage, my stomach cramping and convulsing in horrific pain. I laid there, pleading for it to stop, until my vision went black. Thankfully, I woke about an hour later, my heart slowed down, my body and clothes cold from cooling sweat, my stomach feeling tight and tired but no longer cramping, and having left a pretty recognizable fetal-position-shaped-puddle on the carpet. I had taken eight laxatives at once after a binge hoping to get it out. Nothing came out and thankfully I didn't die. That was the end of my experiments with laxatives. But this did not stop me.

-   We didn't have a lock on the single bathroom in the second house my husband and I lived in. So, I found a board that I kept in the linen closet in the bathroom that I could wedge under the doorknob and below my knee at the toilet to prevent him from coming in during a purge. I sometimes would hear the knob turn and feel pressure on the door and would yank my slimy fingers out of my mouth just long enough to garble out, "Just a minute!" then get right back to it.

Ready for it to stop? Only if you're truly ready to quit.

- When my husband started to occasionally question the odd flushing and other sounds coming from the bathroom, I decided to start purging in the shower. Afraid, at first, that it would not all go down the drain, I was pleasantly surprised to find I could easily smash it all through the little grate covering the drain. Yes, with my hands. This wasn't in any way gross to me.

- I did this for years. Shower-purging. I kept a plunger by the shower for occasional backups.

- Once, with a grumbly, untrustworthy stomach, yet unable to deny myself a binge, the force of my self-inflicted hurl caused me to involuntarily shit at the same time. I actually felt grateful for my decision then to do it in the shower. It all washed away. No one knew.

- I didn't know the bathroom always smelled like puke after I purged. I couldn't smell it.

- My husband once took a photo of me while I was throwing up in the shower. I heard him right as the camera clicked and I sent him violently out, thinking (hoping, begging, pleading in my mind) that he hadn't seen what I was doing. That he hadn't just *captured* what I was doing. Afterward, he awkwardly said he was just trying to have some fun snapping a surprise picture of me in the shower. Petrified, I snatched his phone later when he was outside to see the photo. Thankfully it didn't show anything incriminating. Just my naked back as I was leaned over, and so I told myself what he had said was true. *"He doesn't know anything and I just need to get smarter about it."* I was so dumb. There had never been another time, in our entire marriage, where he tried to take a "fun surprise picture" of me while I was in the shower.

- I hated to make dinner for my husband because it would mean we would have to eat together; so I chose often to work late, leave him something to heat up or easily throw together, and I would intentionally come home after he'd gone to bed, then plop down on the couch, order and eat a pizza. Then shower.

- We divorced soon after this routine began. For many good and right reasons. And one very wrong one: the husband was getting in the way of my eating disorder.

- Bulimics most often do, but should not, live alone. It gives us way too much freedom. When I lived alone, I could revert back to the toilet and do it as many times as I wanted. One very awful Saturday night alone, post-divorce, I peaked. Three times, right in a row. Back-to-back. Stuffed to the gills, then purged to an empty pit. In, then immediately back out. Three times in a row. I cried afterward, knowing for just a sliver of a second, how screwed up, broken, and un-loveable I was. This did not stop me.

- For a year, I lived in an apartment alone where the only thing that ever resided in the fridge for more than a day was milk and a jar of Alfredo in some phase of half-finished. If you think that must have been in college, you would be wrong. I was thirty and a successful, young trial attorney.

- I sometimes formed a calloused sore in the right corner of my mouth from a spoon going in and out too many times. I told people it was a cold sore.

- Sometimes, after a horrendous (often back-to-back) wrenching of my gut, my throat would feel like there was something stuck in it. Like a piece of food was still lodged that I couldn't swallow down. I, of course, felt around to see what I could find (I am intimately familiar with the anatomy of my throat), but found nothing. The sensation—probably a swelling of some part—would sometimes partially clog my airway while working out and make it difficult to breathe. It would make me hoarse for a few days and unable to sing. I love to sing. This did not stop me.

- I once had to scale a fence to get back into my apartment complex after a drive-thru binge and found the security gate would not open. I thought my gut had burst when I landed with a thud on the other side and my knees punched into my swollen, distended stomach. It could have, easily. And my biggest fear was not that my gut had almost burst but that, if it had and I couldn't leave or clean up the scene before EMT arrived, then they would find me with an overly-stuffed stomach and all of my disgusting drive-thru remnants in the car—they would know. Everyone would know. This did not stop me.

Are you thoroughly disgusted yet? Amazed that someone so smart and capable could do these things, self-inflict this kind of pain and embarrassment, with such scary and dangerous risks, and yet keep doing it? Trust me. They can and do. I doubt I'm the most radical bulimic out there. Many of these episodes may be regular occurrences for some. *"Please honey. That's child's play. Wait till you have to explain to the ER doc why there's a spoon stuck in your throat."* Maybe. And, if that's your attitude, totally fine, but it is no longer mine. I was very stupid for going down that road and for catering to that sickness for so long. While I don't know what kind of person I would be, or even where in life I would be, if I hadn't chosen that path, the reality of the matter is that I did go down that road. And it did have an impact on me. It is part of who I am, the adult I have become. But I also believe overcoming that weak state of mind and rescuing myself was one of the hardest things I have ever done and I feel like the strongest person I can possibly be because of it. I know I will never find myself again so vulnerable, desperate, or scared that I choose a path that is not healthy for me.

Surviving and overcoming my eating disorder also gave me greater appreciation for how I spend my time now and the things in my life I have accomplished. Now, overwhelmingly grateful that I was given a second chance at life—one that is not saddled with this costly, dangerous secret—I feel like I can accomplish twice what I did before. I have more energy, drive, and ambition. While I will never say I'm glad I had an eating disorder and I will never be proud of the horrible, risky things I did to my amazing body, I cannot avoid the fact that it impacted me. It molded and often controlled me at a time in my life when I was growing the most—from a teenager to an adult. It is part of who I am today. So, I can't ignore it. I won't deny it. But, I have put it behind me and healed. And you can too. An amazing, fulfilling, delicious life awaits.

If you needed any more reason or nudge, here is my last confession. Guy, I hate that you might someday read this ... but all of this is the reason I am able to give you all of those mind-blowing blow jobs. Please remember that and forgive me.

- My ass started falling out. This was late in the game, toward the very end of my bulimia phase. The worst of it. One time I was clenching my muscles so tight while vomiting—making sure to get every single decadent, sinful bite back up—I felt something happen to my asshole. Like something squished out. I finished (naturally, it is rare that anything will stop us mid-purge until we've rid our body of every single bite), washed up then proceeded to pull down my pants to check what was once my pretty, cute little asshole. Now it was mangled. I had a big pink mass bulging out on the left side of my sphincter. To this day I have no idea what it is. A polyp maybe? A hemorrhoid? A wayward blob of sphincter muscle? I have no clue. But it was right there under the lining: a bulbous, marble-sized ball jutting out the side. I touched it, fearing it might burst but thinking if it was filled with liquid maybe I could somehow drain it. I was prepared to do that. This thought did not gross me out. To be honest, not much involving my body did or probably ever will. But, it was hard and moved around under my skin. I tried to push it back and it would stay swallowed up for a few seconds, then slowly come bulging back out and an instant panic set in. *"I fucked up my asshole! My cute little asshole."* And I wasn't sure if I was going to be able to go number two now, with it bulging out, whether it would ever go back in, or whether more would come popping out if I continued binging and purging, eventually making my asshole look like a budding pink cauliflower. Can you imagine your boyfriend seeing that from behind and still wanting to have sex with you?

With all of those gross, panicky thoughts, this did not stop me.

Thankfully, fear of a cauliflower garden coming out of my ass was frightening and irreversible enough to at least *begin* to nurture the thought that this had to stop. I *had* to stop. I had to find a way to once-and-for-all quit doing this. But, it would be another six months and another horrific bodily experience before I would actually decide to quit, before I was strong enough to finally make and keep that promise to myself. In the meantime, I had my own personal thermometer that would pop out when I puked. *Ding! All done!* And I would then lick my finger and stick it back in.

Yes, I know that's disgusting. Don't be me.

**CHAPTER TWELVE**

# FINALE ONE: INFECTION

It started with an infection. In my mind. Telling me this was okay. This was not such a bad thing to do. *"See? She does it, too. It's fine."* Yet I knew, deep down, when some of those horrendous things I mentioned above would occur—along with about 349 moments that similarly shook me but did not stop me—that it was not fine. It was not okay. It was stupid and dangerous and I needed to stop. But those are weak, fleeting thoughts when trying to stand up against my mental infection. Thankfully, I did have a moment when I finally realized just how sick I was. It was like the first spade jammed in the soil that cut the root of that gnarly vine growing at the base of my neck. It was the first time, of several, where I vividly remember the feeling of stepping outside of my own skin and seeing the moment as a bystander. Seeing myself from the outside, as the version of me I knew (but often refused to admit) that I was: sick.

Thankfully, in this moment it wasn't I who was physically sick. It was Charlene. But it was enough of a snap-to moment for me to embrace the take-away lesson and finally start to see my disease in the harsh light of day. I hope it was for Charlene as well. And all I can do is hope because the very tight bond Charlene and I had created was just another one of the relationships we were both about to lose as a result of our eating disorder. I will never know if this moment had as much of an impact on Charlene, as we didn't see or speak much after it, then not at all after the end of that year. I hope and wonder often whether Charlene was finally able to overcome her illness, too. I will likely never know because, unless she opens up about it like I have (which is rare, even for recovered bulimics), whatever face she puts out to the public will never convey or disclose it.

It was the first of the last three years I would spend crippled by my addiction. Charlene and I, while still friends, had just been spun through a rather twisted love triangle (well, a square really—that's another book) and had ended, when it all blew up, on opposite sides of the ring. So our relationship was already strained and threadbare, likely to soon snap. Then Charlene had to go to the hospital. Nothing related to or caused by her eating disorder, initially, but for a procedure that would unearth and expose her illness for many to see.

Charlene had to have her wisdom teeth removed. A very normal thing for many. Perhaps a bit abnormal to have all four removed at once, but still not uncommon and not anything that was caused by her decision to kneel in front of a toilet and hurl her guts up at least once a day. Ironically, the growth of new teeth in her mouth should have been considered a good thing considering how she treated the current set. But, they were coming in painfully and awkwardly and needed to be removed.

Myself and a few other friends took Charlene to and from the hospital that day, picked up her medications, and spent some time with her at home while she recovered. While she and I never talked about it (we never *actually talked* about it), the thought had occurred to me that it might be painful for her to throw up for a few days after a tooth removal. It would kind of suck, but it would probably register around a three on a scale to ten of the painful things we are willing to do to ourselves to maintain our addiction. *Some added pain and swelling from our self-induced vomiting? No big deal.*

What I did not realize was that it was not going to just be painful for Charlene to puke, it was going to be altogether impermissible. I know *now*, because of Charlene's episode and having had a wisdom tooth subsequently removed myself—thankfully well after I was in the healing process and capable of going days, weeks even, without falling back into my hole—that there are three "S's" you cannot do the first few days after a tooth is removed: straw, smoke, or suck. While the smoking ban is just obvious—nothing will heal well while choking in a cloud of smoke—the straw and suck bans are necessary because the cavity where your tooth once was needs to clot and heal and a sucking force in your mouth can break or remove the clot, preventing healing. Obviously, violent torrents of stomach contents erupting from your throat and exiting out through your mouth would not only rip the clots out, but replace the gaping hole with vile stomach acids and infection-causing food particles. Throwing up is not just a bad impulse you should try to avoid after a tooth removal, it is something you are not permitted to do.

I did not know this at the time. A smart, thirty-two-year-old lawyer, should I have? Probably. It would be obvious for most people. But bulimics are not most people, and the thought of something occurring in our lives that would prevent us from being able to throw up does not just casually cross our minds.

In telling this story of Charlene's four-tooth removal, which is graphic and rather tragic, there are two incredibly funny moments I feel I have to share. While this book is intended to help both you and myself recover, in doing so, I think we all need to be able to laugh at ourselves every now and then. Otherwise, you'll take yourself so seriously, nothing will ever get through. So, the first: Bandaged to High Heaven.

"What did you say?" I asked her, because whatever had just come muffled out of her mouth sounded like: "Thidit aspen det?" It was definitely a question, the end of the sentence careening upward in the form of an inquiry. But it sounded nothing like English.

Charlene sat propped up in her bed, four bags of ice packed around her jaws with a fat gauze bandage wrapped round and round her chin and up over the top of her head, like a cartoon character in the infirmary. Her cheeks were puffed out like a chipmunk, with thick cotton logs protruding from her mouth. It was hard to look at her and not laugh. Thankfully you could do that while she was asleep. Charlene had fallen asleep immediately after we got her home and in bed. Still loopy from the meds and hurting at the hospital, she hadn't said anything during the drive home. Now, a few hours later, she was just starting to wake and rouse and those were her first words:

"Thidit aspen det?" I was still perplexed.

"I'm sorry, Charlene, I can't understand you. One more time," I encouraged her and this time she decided to add helpful hand signals.

Charlene pointed to her bandage-wrapped, cotton-stuffed head and asked, a little more clearly this time: "Did thit appen yet?" Finally it clicked for me and I covered my mouth with my hand to try and hide my shocked smile.

"Are you asking me 'Did it happen yet?'" I asked Charlene, my eyes wide with disbelief, my teeth biting down my devious lips.

Charlene bobbed her gauze helmet up and down a few times in a nod of yes, her eyes begging for an answer. And then I finally just had to laugh.

"Yes, Charlene. It happened. They took your wisdom teeth out," I told her as I patted her shoulder and watched her eyes roll back to sleep.

But I couldn't help laughing again as I clicked the door shut and left her room thinking to myself: *"I mean, Jesus, Darling, do you wake up like this often? Bandaged to high heaven, your mouth full of cotton and your head thumping in pain? Is this a common state you find yourself in the morning after? What do your nights at the bar look like, lady? Of course, it happened!"*

I was still laughing about it, when re-enacting it for Charlene at the bar later. Thankfully, alcohol didn't seem to be one of those naughty "S's" you had to avoid after a tooth removal. No one seemed to frown upon a cocktail after the procedure, so Charlene and I were downing her toothaches away with permissible pitcher after pitcher of sangrias. As long as you didn't drink it through a straw, right? Well, Charlene didn't;

because she had another use for that straw. Cue the second moment: Happy Hour at Tiffany's.

Charlene, unfortunately, had two addictions: puking and smoking. She had been "trying to quit" (the latter, not the former, are you crazy?) since I met her, but not very successfully. As you know, many smokers claim "I only smoke when I drink." While that is usually never true—that same "Drink-Only Smoker" is going to wake the next morning and light at least one up as part of their morning ritual and we all know it—it is true that believing you are or actually *being* a person who "only smokes when they drink" only encourages you to drink more and more often. Meaning, a "drink-only smoker" is not a status that's really any better than being an openly-admitted smoker. But stubbornly continuing to call herself a "drink-only smoker," this post-tooth-removal ban on smoking was causing Charlene some serious grief, particularly as we were now, sitting at the bar, drinking. But Charlene had a solution. Us bulimics, I tell you. We are crafty.

Assuming the problem with smoking while you have four gaping holes in your mouth is that allowing smoke in and around said holes, as opposed to clean oxygen, will hinder their ability to heal, then the solution is rather easy. Bypass the holes. I will never forget watching Charlene, her face still puffy and swollen (but with her gauze helmet at least removed), lighting a cigarette stuck in the end of a straw, the other end shoved deep in her mouth, all the way back to her throat. Her thinking being if she could get the smoke past the bloody holes and straight to her throat to be inhaled, then exhale through the nose and there would be no problem. The reality that Charlene was now breaking not one, but two, of the almighty "S's" by smoking *through* a straw was all too obvious, but a part of me felt her thinking was sound. And seeing her then, looking like a redneck version of Audrey Hepburn in *Breakfast at Tiffany's*, part of me was a little proud.

That changed a few days later. It was one of our last encounters and definitely the last night Charlene and I spent out drinking together. That first night after she had her wisdom teeth removed, Charlene simply didn't eat anything at all. That was easy. As I mentioned, part of being a functioning bulimic is the ease with which we can deny ourselves food. We actually have a desire to do it, so that our desire for it grows stronger and the hunger builds, making our delicious fix all the more satisfying. But if we decide to withhold food, we must, at some point, get that fix.

Two days after Charlene had her wisdom teeth removed, we found ourselves back at the bar after a long, exceedingly stressful day at the office. I remember I'd had a deposition that day. I had deposed an expert in a medical malpractice case and I was incredibly disappointed in myself. I had let the other attorney bully me around and I hadn't fought back as hard as I should have. As a result, he had trampled me with objections and intimidated me into changing or withholding questions I should have asked, I was supposed to ask. I was pissed off at myself and looking to spend the night drinking my anger down. I also knew after our time at the bar, that I would then eat my anger, and throw up my anger, and that it was the only thing that would help my anger subside.

But it did not. I was more angry and disappointed in myself after I threw up that night than I ever could have been in that stupid deposition. It was the first time I made myself sit and stare into my pink puddle of filth, smelling it, acknowledging it, for minutes, half an hour maybe. I don't know. But I forced myself to sit there, till the vomit and snot dried on my face. Till I felt my own teeth had decayed a little from the acidic slime in my mouth. I couldn't believe what I had seen that night, the angry beast that screamed at me, and yet I still did it. I was that weak. I was that small.

An hour before, I had been with Charlene. We'd successfully quieted both of our stressed, angry legal minds with more than a few drinks and were having fun hiking our skirts up and talking circles around guys at the bar. Everything was normal, right on track for just another drunken night out, which was usually followed by our respective ridiculous routines once we were back at home alone: flush, never happened, wake up, repeat, see you at the bar tomorrow. Everything was fine. For me. I hadn't realized the past few days had left Charlene clawing at herself, wanting desperately to eat, which she could perfectly well do with the holes in her jaw nearly healed, but she could perfectly well *not do* the way she was wanting to— to get that release, that endorphin rush from binging and that heart-thumping high when it all comes exquisitely back out—by eating massive, satisfying quantities then throwing them up. I hadn't realized Charlene had spent the past few days facing her demon, trying to block out the cacophonous shrieks in her head shouting: *"Eat! Don't eat! Do it. Let go! Hold it together. Don't do it! Keep it down! THROW IT UP!"*

At the time, I could only imagine what that must have sounded like. Now I know, as I have since faced and slapped and kicked and spat at my own demon, who was shouting the same things, but sadly this night did not stop me. It only started the change. It was the first shovel in the dirt.

Charlene began to spiral at the bar. She was very drunk, which meant her raw emotions, the ones she usually kept buried under thick layers of secrecy, wit, and beauty were starting to show. Charlene started snapping at me and others around her, ordering stronger drinks, and even slapping a guy who tried to help her as she stumbled off her stool and stormed to the bathroom. I smoothed things over and paid our tab at the bar, knowing it was high time for the two of us to go to our separate purge pads. But, I wasn't ready for what I found in the bathroom.

Charlene was leaning against the wall with her back to me, punching herself in the stomach. When she heard the door shut she turned around to face me. Her face was violently red, black streaks of mascara streaming from her eyes, her nostrils flaring with each hot breath. She started walking toward me, her hands white-knuckled, balled in tight fists. I honestly thought she might hit me but I just stood there as she got face to face with me and screamed at the top of her lungs, spit flying from her lips:

"ALL I WANT TO DO IS THROW UP!"

I stood there, staring at her. My eyes darting from one eye to the other, finally seeing what we had both become and now knowing that many people at the bar might know. We were vile creatures that needed daily feeding, who could not function without our drug. I couldn't, as I stood there, have imagined going three days without doing it. The torture that would cause me. I wouldn't know what to eat or how to stop myself from binging. I wouldn't know how to pass that time, how to quiet that beast, how to do anything else that would give me that necessary release. I would have done exactly what Charlene was doing: punching myself and screaming.

I was her. She was me. We were both so infected and we knew it.

I don't know if it was caused by the smoking, the drinking, the Straw at Tiffany's attempt or if Charlene finally caved and threw up that night anyway. My guess is the latter. I'm sure she threw up. Probably right about the same time I did that night after we both left the bar. As I mentioned, our relationship was already unthreading at the time, and I think that moment in the bathroom told the both of us, our bond was not healthy. I only saw Charlene a handful of times after that, always in a crowd that didn't allow us to really talk about anything, especially that night. But I know that whatever the cause, Charlene developed dry socket in all four of her wisdom cavities.

It was the first time I had ever heard of "dry socket" and I learned it is an incredibly painful exposure of the bone and nerve in the cavities due to a failure to form a healing clot, and that it can lead to a deep, painful, and debilitating infection in the jaw. I also heard through mutual friends that Charlene's case was very bad, lasting several weeks, and requiring her to go to an oral surgeon to have the painfully-exposed cavities re-packed, which I was sure would mean she would again have to go another period of time without throwing up. If she could. While I hated to think of a friend suffering so badly, my only hope was it would ultimately serve to cure Charlene of the horrendous disease we both suffered from.

I realized—both in that moment in the bathroom with Charlene and later, while staring at and letting my own mouth drip into the filth in the toilet—I was sick, too. Just as infected as Charlene was with this twisted addiction and it had to stop. I'll bet if Charlene did throw up that night as well—which I am quite sure she did—she, too, made herself sit and stare at her own puddle of filth. And I would have to imagine how painful that must have been for her to make herself throw up with four raw, bleeding holes in her mouth and that afterward her hand, face, and puddle was swirled with thick, red blood. I can use these mental images now to tamp back the occasional craving, but it wasn't enough for me then. The hold was still too strong. Even though I would soon find myself staring at my own bloody contents in a disgusting bowl and my own bloody, slimy face in the mirror afterward—so much blood drained out of me that I was almost too weak to stand—this too would not yet stop me; because finally realizing you are addicted and deciding you "want" to stop or that you "should" stop is a far cry from deciding I AM STOPPING RIGHT NOW. This minute. That was the last time. Then *actually* stopping. All of those are exceedingly harder. Unfortunately, the most difficult times for me, still remained ahead.

Breaking an addiction is never easy, but it can be done. You are stronger than that red-faced demon screaming in the bathroom.

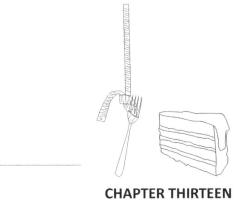

**CHAPTER THIRTEEN**

# FINALE TWO: CATHARSIS

Ca·thar·sis (*noun*): the process of releasing, and thereby providing relief from, strong or repressed emotions.

I was surprised when I saw this definition. Like Ole' Webster knew me better than I knew myself. I had always heard catharsis was an ancient form of remedy where doctors would cut a patient and let blood drain out in the belief the illness would drain along with it. I never knew it was also considered a release of repressed emotions. If there is any better analogy for causing yourself to throw up, that would be it. *"Puke all that fear, pain, and worry out and everything will be just fine."* Right. Because that works.

Catharsis was the first word I thought of when I saw it: a huge river of red flowing into the bowl. Like most other bulimics, you probably close your eyes for most of the process. I mean, it's not like you're going to miss the bowl. It's a pretty big target when your face is that close and—let's face it—you're pretty good at aiming your own vomit. (I was still jockeying for that Golden Toilet Award.) But, just for another disgusting detail— you also close your eyes to prevent potential backsplash from getting into your eyes. Your face, hair, and shoulders are fine. That's a quick clean-up. Clothes are a bit more of a problem, which is why I'm sure many of you probably take your top off before doing it.

Is it gross I know these things? Yes, very. But it proves I know what you do and how you do it. And, how you can stop. Wait until you hear this:

That was the first word that conjured in my mind: *"Catharsis."* I was performing my own blood-letting. Not intentionally, mind you. I can't say what caused it, other than the obvious—the immense pressure that roars through my head each time I hurl. But mid-way through my session I, for whatever reason, opened my eyes for a moment and was surprised by it: the quantity of blood that was in the toilet. Then I looked at my hand and saw it there, too. A slimy trail of bright red blood starting at my knuckles and creeping down my wrist. At first I thought maybe I had cut my knuckle vomiting, but surely I would have felt that. And, let's face it, I was a pro. I had never cut a knuckle throwing up in my life. Then the thought occurred to me:

*My nose must be bleeding.*

I stood up from the toilet so I could make my way to the mirror. Yes, mid-session. Yes, irritated at the moment for my decision to stop the process mid-way because I knew this would make it harder to pick back up and get everything out, but I had to know. Then I saw it. Staring at me in the mirror. I looked like a raging, mutant bull. My face and neck red and bulging with the effort and two thick streams of blood pouring from my nose to my chin, now dripping onto my bare chest. I wonder now, as I write this, if any of the people in my life would still see me the same way if they saw what I saw in the mirror that day. It was worse than Charlene's black tear-streamed face in the bathroom. Way worse. I was bloody and slimy and ugly. In a *Lifetime* teenage movie about my eating disorder this would be the moment that I punched the mirror into shards and stopped being bulimic right then and there. *"Take that big, bad disease!"*

But this is not a *Lifetime* movie. This is real life. And, we're far too addicted for just one horrific image to stop us.

I went back to the toilet. To finish, of course. Nothing else mattered. Struggling, just as I knew I would, to get the compulsion back, get my reflux working again so I could eject everything out; and in doing so, you can only imagine what the tight squeeze of my muscles and the pressure it caused in my head did to my bleeding nose. Do you know what happens when you throw up with a bloody nose? I did not then, but I do now. You hemorrhage. Each wicked convulsion of your body that squeezes your stomach to eject its contents also squeezes the blood out of every vein in your head. I had a red river flowing just as swiftly as my vomit into the bowl. My hand was covered in blood and gut slime, the coppery taste and smell of it almost making me heave out of repulsion every time I kept jamming it back in my throat. But I kept jamming it in.

This time I did it all with my eyes open, watching blood pour in a red, violent river from my face. Once I did finally start throwing up again, it got worse. Blood was pouring out in alarming quantities, splattering the walls and floor. The contents in the bowl were now more red than pink and while I knew I had gotten pretty much everything out, I always pushed for that last little bit. Until all that came out was one vile drop of acid. I had to get *there*. Or I wasn't yet done.

Was this my most disgusting moment: kneeled like a sad, sick girl next to a murder scene of a toilet? Yes. Well, or equivalent, at least, to my shitty shower scene. But, did this stop me? No.

My only thought in continuing was that I hoped I could get all of my stomach contents out before I bled enough to pass out. While dying is an unlikely outcome from just a nose bleed, the thought didn't occur to me then that if the pressure was so great to cause the veins in my nose to break at random and bleed, it might also be enough to cause my gut to bust or my throat to rip open. Thankfully for me, my strong, capable, beautiful body held it together long enough for me to get better without permanent damage. But, I remember thinking during that particular purge session that I'd better hurry and get it all out before I bled to death. Or worse, bled just enough to make me pass out in a pool of vile snot, blood, and puke, and be *discovered* like that. To have the person you want the least to know, to then *know*.

That would be worse than dying. Way worse.

And that should tell you everything you need to know. What is the thing that finally stopped me? The only thing I believe is strong enough to reach us? Shame. A moment when I was almost discovered. When he was about to *know.*

# CHAPTER FOURTEEN

# FINALE THREE: SHAME

These would be my drive-thru days. Boy, did I spend an alarming amount of money and time going through drive-thrus and eating. In case you're curious, let's just go there. This was my usual route and order:

First stop, Whataburger: A patty melt meal, add two pieces of cheese ("to make four total on the burger," because I always had to tell them this), onion rings instead of fries with white chicken gravy to dip them in, a large milkshake as my drink and add a large water. Gotta get those stomach contents creamed up like a smoothie.

Next up, Krystal: I would commence eating the patty melt and rings while driving there (I am a pro at steering with my knees), then order three corn pups with extra ketchup ("like, ten ketchup packs total," I would have to tell them), and loaded chili cheese fries.

Stop number three, Taco Bell: I had usually finished the patty melt and started dipping the corn pups into the ketchups I had squeezed into the empty Whataburger gravy cup on my way to Taco Bell. ("How" you might ask? The knees!) I would then order a cheese quesadilla, two burrito supremes and a twelve-pack of the Cinnabon delights. "The twelve pack, not the four," I would always have to tell them. "And four sides of nacho cheese," for pouring onto each bite of the burritos. "Yes, four, total. Four little cups of nacho cheese," I would always have to tell them.

And with the exception of the occasional leftover bites or buns, I could usually eat all of this—in just one session. My stomach would be distended to the point of rupture. Walking from the car back to the apartment often found me in severe pain. With that much food trying to make its way through my body, I would sometimes have to "go" so badly I would have to stop in the stairwell and sit hard on my ankle to hold it back. When this would occur and after I'd emptied my body from both ends my sick self would think: *Oh goodie, two outs. I'm even skinnier now! Gold stars!*

If you are feeling just about as embarrassed and stupid as I am now, you're welcome.

What was good about the drive-thru method, though, was that all the binging took place in the solitude of my car. I'm sure I got some strange looks from people driving next to me on the road when they saw all of the burger wrappers, bags, and napkins that littered the front seat. Not to mention *me* stuffing my face behind the wheel. I didn't care. They were strangers. *"Screw you, I'm hungry!"*

I often had the occasional drive-thru attendee catch me with my mouth so full, my teeth covered in tortilla and my mouth swaddled with some concoction of cheese, ketchup, and gravy, that I couldn't say "thank you" when they handed me my *next* bag of grease, or those extra ten ketchups I had asked for. I just wiped my chipmunk-looking mouth and nodded at them. I'm sure they knew, but I didn't care. *"Screw you too, I'm hungry!"* my warped mind said.

Sadly, I made these rounds so often that I began to start seeing the same fast food workers at these joints and they knew my stupid, custom order. I mean, each was a very odd, strange order, so my brilliant response was to start making jokes about it. "Oh, you know the guys at the office. They'll be pissed if I don't come with those extra nacho cheeses." Although I'm sure the half-eaten pile of crap I was trying to hide in the front passenger seat, not to mention my puffed out cheeks and ketchup-stained shirt, betrayed me. Those drive-thru people knew.

I was so stupid. And about to be broke, too, continuing at that pace. Buying all of that crap sometimes cost me in the neighborhood of forty dollars per round. This is for stuff I just shoved in my face and threw back up. An experience so disgusting and embarrassing, I was willing to pay for it! It's like walking up to someone and handing them a twenty-dollar bill so they can punch you in the mouth. Jesus, how much money, time, spit, and saliva (gross!) I spent during my drive-thru days. But, at least I can say it was the last phase of my eating disorder. I am now happily in Healthy Phase and loving every minute so much more. But how did I get here?

There was a little mention of a love triangle back there wasn't there? Or square, rather. I know you haven't forgotten. How did

Charlene and I first get sideways?

Over a guy, of course. But not in the way you might think. This was *the* guy. My now guy. My partner, mate, lover, best friend, and forever adventure buddy. He is the most important person in my life. And, while I cringe as I write this (at home, alone, as just my little secret) knowing he will likely someday read it, I know this book needs to be and must be published. My story needs to reach some of you because I truly think the honest, disgusting truth has to be told to you by someone who was there. Hunched over the toilet just like you, heaving pink blood-chunky rivers into the toilet just like you, and who is here, shouting at you now, telling you that you can stop. That you *have* to stop. It will be better on the other side for you, too. I promise.

But, while this is not the particular story I would like to share with *him*, this disease—both the development of it and my conquering of it, an accomplishment of which I am extremely proud—it is all part of who I am, and I believe he will see and understand that. And, continue to hold my hand even after he knows where time and again it's been. Trust me, he knew "for a time there, I was bulimic," but he does not know how long it went on—well after he and I were living together—and some of the truly repulsive things I did to hide and continue it. But, that is my cross to bear. And I believe in him, as well as this book. Because mostly, I believe in you—whoever is reading this. If you're trying to quit, I know that you can, and I know this book can help. My guy will see that too.

So, back to the triangle. Or square.

After the divorce I obviously started dating again. And, we'll just call it what it was at first—fucking random guys for fun. Usually Navy guys. Usually twenty-something, ten-years-younger-than-me guys. Because, for a while, that can be fun and confidence-boosting. Assuming the guys are good lays and not clingy and you don't let your heart get into the mix. For a time, it was fun. And it fit nicely with my solitary life and my sick routine. No guy who just wants to fuck you really cares whether you've had dinner or don't keep any food at your house. There's a roof. There's a bed. Boom. It's done. Then he's gone and you're left to indulge whatever other cravings you might have. But, that changes when you meet someone you want to do more than that with. Someone who crawls under your skin, seeps into your thoughts, and starts to bring out something new in you. Love is a very volatile, dangerous, beautiful thing and when it happens, there's no un-doing it. It's done. You want to be around that person more and it will hurt if that cannot happen.

But, unless you've found a partner who wants to sit on the couch and stuff his or her face with doughnuts alongside you (God, I hope not), your together time will start to encroach on your dirty little secret. Meals will start to pose problems. And you may actually push someone out of your life who loves you very much, because you love food more. I'm sure that's happened for many of you.

I was greedier than you. I wanted them both.

And having them both was easy in the beginning, when Guy and I still lived in separate apartments and only saw each other three or four nights a week. On the bright side, I did begin eating healthier with him. And by that, I don't mean simply eating half of an actual, regular person meal and keeping it down. Guy is very health-conscience, and a wonderful chef with a focus on farm-to-table organic foods; his meals are not only incredibly delicious, but exceptionally healthy. For the first time in years, I had begun eating—with him—the occasional, complete, normal adult meals. Baby steps. Love was slowly bringing me out of my dark, dirty cave. Yet, I still maintained my binge-and-purge routine when I was alone because: a) I liked doing it (I'm that sick freak); and b) I didn't know how to shop for good ingredients and prepare my own healthy meals at home. So, there was no other way to eat healthy apart from him. I truly believed this.

But, as I began to spend more time with Guy, I got healthier in many ways. I wasn't spending as much time in the evenings at the bar, drinking heavily and trolling for guys. I was no longer sleeping with random strangers, anyone of whom could carry a host of lifelong STD's. (And for that, my pussy thanks me.) I also wasn't binging and purging as much, because Guy and I were often together three or four nights a week as well as the entire weekend. This began to enable me to temper my cravings more to where I could now go three or more days without going there, without doing *that*. Because I would rather be with him. It also forced me to pull away from Charlene, which was, I think we both knew it even at the time, a good thing. Encouraging, even cheering, each other toward the same goal—skinny through disease, the Golden Toilet Award!—Charlene and I were not a healthy pairing. But, that was not what initially sheared our bond.

Charlene had actually introduced me to Guy. He was a friend of a man she was dating rather seriously at the time and the introduction was made in hopes the four of us—cue the square—could happily double-date and hang out, go out, or even travel eventually, as buddy couples. This was our happy status for a brief stint, then some bad shit went down between Charlene and her guy. Something she believed he had done (which later turned out, as he swore time and time again in the face of her vicious accusations, he had not), but which caused a drawn-out, overly-dramatic, tear-jerking split between Charlene and her guy, which Charlene did not handle well at all. She was wrecked, on a warpath (out to hurt only herself, mind you, to punish herself for what *she* had allowed to happen in her life: to be hurt by a boy), and she wanted a fellow warrior. Much happier and healthier than the state Charlene had found me in two years prior and growing closer to my guy and a healthy normal life with him, I was not willing to pick up the shield and blaze the bars alongside her every night. This hurt Charlene deeply, infuriated her to the point (I learned later) that she tried to get my guy to do what she believed hers had in a sad, desperate attempt to get me back.

She's lucky I learned this well after she and I had severed our ties and she moved out of state, or damn if I wouldn't have pulled every other tooth in her head out and left her with a mouth full of dry sockets! But bulimics are a desperate bunch. We ravage our bodies over and over again because we're often filled with rage, anger, and fear (of losing control of our lives) and our attempt to violently hurl those emotions out of our body like bile is just that: desperate. And futile. Whatever inner demon you have raging inside of you that you believe you can quiet, at least for a moment, when you start stuffing your face with food, he will be back as soon as you finish and start getting hungry again.

He shouts and screams and claws at you while you're pacing the kitchen, opening and closing the refrigerator door, trying to tell yourself not to do it. Then he quiets down when you finally cave and shove that first bite of frosted cake into your face because he's now laughing at you. You cracked. You fell. You're weak. He'll wait until you think you're a little stronger. That you don't have an uncontrollable addiction, that you can *not do it* anytime you want to. *"Right,"* he says. *"Sure,"* he says. Then he'll start his scratching, and whispering, and clawing, and shouting again. Your sick routine fuels him because it keeps pulling you back to that weak state where he loves to see you, kneeled over a vomit-splattered toilet. He probably has pictures of you in various states of that condition framed on his walls. And when that craving starts and you try to argue against it, he just points to one and says: *"Shush now. This will be you in an hour."* He taunts you with this.

Don't let him!

Like I did. The photo he had of me the time my nose bled while I was throwing up—the murder scene toilet—was probably his favorite. But, sadly for me, I was too weak to let it be his last. Losing Charlene and the bond she and I shared—her being the only other person in the entire world who knew and shared my secret, who I could actually talk to about that if I reached a breaking point—was more discomforting than I would like to admit. I felt far more alone in the world. And while my guy and I were growing closer and I was eating far healthier than I ever had with his glorious cooking, I was still mentally sick. Food was still a problem, something to be shunned at some times, gorged at others. I hadn't yet admitted to myself that I was sick and had a demon to face and a decision to make. This meant, when left alone for long periods of time, even after moving in with him, I was still very much capable (and willing) to cave and bow to my monster. Often, when I knew for sure Guy would be gone long enough and there was enough soft-serve type stuff in the house that I didn't think he would notice was missing, or that I could replace before he did notice, I would do it. Then hide it.

While 99% of the time, Guy did not sense anything was up, occasionally, I would slip and this would lead to a very weird conversation between Guy and I when I would get caught in an awkward food lie:

Guy: "So, what did you have for lunch, babe?"
Me: "Oh, I went to that new vegetarian place on 9th."
Guy: "Oh, really? I thought they were closed on Mondays."
Me: "Huh, guess not."
*[Insert my abrupt and suspicious subject-change here.]*

Guy: "What did you have for lunch, babe?"
*I hated that question.*
Me: "Oh, the leftover chicken and rice that was in the fridge."
*Which I had actually dumped into a jar, shoved inside a box, inside a bag in the trash right before I binged on mac and cheese instead.*
Guy: "Callie, we made that last week. Are you sure it was still good? You have to be careful with leftover rice."
Me: "You know me! An iron gut!"
*[Insert another abrupt and suspicious subject-change by me here.]*

Guy: "So, what did you have for lunch, babe?"
*"Racha fracka ..."* I would curse under my breath.
Me: "Oh, I was super busy. Just had some carrots and hummus. What's for dinner?"
*Here I'm trying to be healthy, because that's honestly what I ate... after I had binged on pasta and I honestly was excited and looking forward to sharing a healthy dinner with Guy.*

Guy: "Well ... " he would start in, puzzled while picking through the pantry. "I was going to say chicken piccatta because I swear we had a whole box of angel hair pasta in here."

*"Oh you did,"* I would think to myself. *"Before I ate it all, buried in two jars of Aflredo. Dammit Callie!"* I would curse myself for slipping.

Me: "Huh, I don't know where it went, babe. You know me. Carbs aren't really my thing."

*[Insert my abrupt and suspicious subject-change here.]*

The problem was I hadn't yet had that "talk with myself." And you can get all *Lifetime* movie with it and stand dramatically in front of the mirror and say it out loud, if that's the flare you think will make it work. But at some point, you have to admit you are sick and that you take stress and pain and fear and whatever other emotions, when they pile too high in your head and overwhelm you, and you shove it all down your throat, then you throw it all back up. That's how you deal with those emotions and now you're going to stop. You're going to tell somebody, get accountable, find another way to cope, and you're going to get better.

Until you have that talk and, not just make that pact with yourself but actually keep that pact, actually *do those things*— stop, tell someone, and find another coping mechanism—even if you haven't binged in weeks, you're still that person. The one who sees your secret as not that bad of a thing. The one who craves three cheeseburgers in a row. The one who, when you get angry, or worried, or bored, or hurt, the one thing you think will truly make you feel better is three cheeseburgers in a row. Until you un-become that person by letting your secret out and holding yourself accountable, the next time something bad, or scary, or hurtful in your life happens (because it will, whether you're skinny or beautiful or fat or ugly or nothing like whatever you're seeing in your head), that's the first place you will go and you'll spiral back into a relapse. Trust me, I've done that, too. Many times.

*I've done everything baby. Twenty years solid at this.* But, at this point in my timeline I was about to stop. Things were about to change, because I finally hit the brick-wall that knocked the breath out of my lungs, the food out of my hand, and the desire out of my gut to ever do that again. For many of you, there is probably only one thing that can hit you that hard. That can scare you into finally changing. It's what you feel if you've ever come close to being discovered. Your roommate comes home early and almost catches you binging, your spouse almost comes into the bathroom to find you making yourself throw up: What is the one hot, panicky, heart-penetrating feeling you have in that moment?

SHAME.

Having frequent cramps and stomach pain obviously doesn't bother you enough to stop. Having to clean the filthy splatters from the walls, the floor, your face doesn't really bother you. Having to live forever alone and constantly turn down social invitations that might (*don't say it!*) involve food doesn't really bother you. Severing ties or distancing yourself from people who care about and love you because they tried to help you change and get healthy is not really a big deal. The only thing that scares you about this disease is people—with whom you love, live, work with, or respective, people you want to continue to respect you—finding out. The thought of them learning you are a filthy, weak creature who doesn't deserve to be loved, respected, or admired makes your blood spike through your skin.

The shame of what you do is what makes you go to such great lengths and lies to hide it. And as long as its hidden and no one knows, you can keep doing it. Going *there* when you've had a rough day. Doing *that* when the stress of your life roars in your head like a dragon. Trust me. I know. And I hope the reality of all of this is starting to sink in. But more than that, I hope that shameful moment happens to you. I truly do.

That's right. I'm not your bulimia buddy here. I'm not here to help you continue doing this, help you hide it and keep feeding that demon. I'm here to be that brick-wall moment. In case you are never discovered or you never have that heart-pumping moment when you are almost discovered, I'm hoping you can relate to my journey enough to experience my moment with me. And then finally stop.

I change my answer about the favorite photo. I actually think the one my demon liked the most was my face when I thought I had been caught—utterly and inexplicably caught. My repugnant secret witnessed by the one person in the world I would never want to see me like that: Guy. Along with several of his business partners, whom I also worked for at the time. Men who think I am a smart, capable woman, worthy of their trust and respect. The face they would have seen in that moment conveyed anything but.

Considering the number of times I did it—made myself throw up—the number of times when I was living with someone and almost got caught were far and few between, particularly in my later days, because I was so good at both doing it and hiding it.

So programmed and calculated and disciplined about it. Rarely was there any piece of trash or a trace left, not even a smell or a hint. But, I did have my moments when my roommate came home early and I had to throw everything away in a flash, jump in the bathroom, lock the door and turn on the shower to mask my guttural heaves. When a colleague or client wanted an urgent immediate meeting while I was half-way through a patty melt on my second drive-thru stop, and I had to hide the gulping sounds I made while trying to swallow so I could speak clearly and come up with some believable reason why I needed thirty minutes before I could make the meeting. Sure, I had a few of those.

One of the most hilarious? (Well, *now* it's funny. At the moment, it was almost a death knell for me.) One night, after drinking and whooping it up on the town, I was the DD and Guy had a wild hair to get a late fast food craving fix on the way home. No problem. He knew I wouldn't touch a bite of that stuff for many reasons. In his mind, I never eat fast food because that's junk food that turns straight to fat. Little did he know, I ate a ton of it, I just didn't keep it down. It's also a burger. Because I hadn't had that talk with myself yet—finally mending my horrible relationship with food—I was still very much that girl from the back cover, and all of these things Guy knew and they were a very true and accurate synopsis of my approach to food at that time. I didn't eat burgers because they are junk food. I also didn't eat them because they have bread on them. *Carbs? Are you crazy?* It was also around 2:00 a.m., and I didn't eat anything after dinner. Never dessert. *Sweets? Are you crazy?*

Poor Guy. I really do hate all of those years I missed, all of those fun meals and moments we could have shared together, which we do now, because my wires were so crossed when it came to food. Throw food into the mix and everything got weird for Callie. But, Guy was very patient with me, thinking for years I was just like many other girls: always carefully watching my figure and picky about food so I could maintain a good physique. That's not such a bad thing to endure but I know he felt a little lonely sometimes when I refused a single bite of something indulgent he was eating that he just wanted to share with me.

If you read this: *Guy, I'm sorry.*

And here we were again, both of us healthy, very fit and very capable of sharing a late night burger without it doing anything but good for us. I mean we had danced all night, likely burning way more calories than half a burger would amount to. But, I was messed up when it came to food. I, of course, declined his offer to split one (although I was probably hungrier than he was) but I offered to happily drive Guy anywhere he wanted to go for his late-night beef fix. A little bummed to be the only one with the craving, but understanding of my many weird ways when it came to food, Guy conceded and announced his burger joint of choice:

"Whataburger," he said.

Instantly I panicked. There was only one Whataburger on our route home and (stupid me!) it was the one I always went to for my fix. The one where the drive-thru gal *knew* me. Where, if I heard her voice come over the intercom, I could've just started with "Yeah, I'd like a patty melt with two extra slices of ..." and she would've interrupted me and said, "Oh it's you!" and completed my weird, indulgent order without another word spoken between us. This was the Whataburger Guy wanted to go to.

*Shit!*

But, it was 2:00 a.m. Surely my "Oh it's you!" gal doesn't work all day *and* pull an all-nighter, I thought to myself. It's likely she won't be there, or I can at least muffle my voice enough and because the order will not be the same, surely she won't recognize me. *Surely*.

Thankfully Guy was at least tipsy enough to not notice I was sweating and fidgeting as we pulled up to the little intercom. I waited, painfully, for the voice to come through ... hoping, praying ... it was not her. Then I heard it and thought to myself:

*"Oh it's you."*

Fuck. It was her. It was most definitely her. "Ummm ... " I stalled. "I ... " I stuttered. Then a thought snapped to.

"You know what?" I turned to Guy, because if I was going to sell this, it had to have a good story. "If you really want a greasy hangover cure, I know what you really need." Guy looked at me curiously. "It's what me and my roommates in college always used to get after a big night out. You know, before we'd go home and have pillow fights in our bras and panties," I said with a smile and a wink.

I may have had a raging eating disorder, but I was still a firecracker.

Throw the cliché all-girls pillow fight in there and any guy, even my Guy, would want to go where the rest of that story is going. I ditched the intercom and drove right through the drive-thru (vowing to myself to never go to *that* Whataburger again) with the window rolled up while I was enthralling Guy with some of my best Girls Gone Wild college day stories while I drove to a nearby, similarly-open-twenty-four-hour-joint knowing exactly what I was going to get him. It was what my college roommates actually did used to get after a bender, but I of course always declined and ordered a Diet Coke. *Because that really gives a hangover the ole' one-two punch.*

But Guy liked my story, it involved me and what I'm sure he thought were girls I experimented with in college, so he was on board. I pulled up to Waffle House with a smile and he followed me in. As we sat at a sticky little bench, I pushed the laminated menus to the side and announced to the waiter who came up with a pad, pen, and a smile: "We'll have the hash browns please. Scattered, covered, and smothered."

Guy was smiling then, and I can't say that I blame him. For the moment, I was not broken. I was his fun, adventurous, spontaneous food buddy and now he had someone to share his late-night grease fest with because there was one thing that could get me to put "bad" things in my mouth, swallow them, and keep them down. And, it was the thought of him discovering my dirty little secret. The shame that would cause me. And that moment finally did come. And I did swallow everything and, for once, finally kept it all down.

It wasn't long after the Whataburger "Oh it's you!" incident because, as I mentioned, if you let yourself fall back into that cave, it screws up your body's natural metabolism. You're not sure when to be hungry, when to eat or how much, what's normal "full" supposed to feel like, what is the right thing to do now to stay skinny while still keeping that paper-thin promise you made to yourself to "try to stop." So, the easiest thing to do is get back on the crazy train and revert back to your old habits: starve yourself most of the day, refusing any indulgences, saving up for one big binge and purge that will tide you over until the next day. As long as you have the freedom to pull it off and keep it hidden, that routine is much easier than trying to make yourself eat and keep down three square meals a day, workout like a normal person, and not fear every minute you're growing fat cells on your thighs. I know how stupid that sounds but it's just the truth. An eating disorder is a brutal mental hold that is very hard to break.

And, I had a schedule and work environment at the time that, unfortunately, really dovetailed nicely with this routine. I was self-employed at the time, living with Guy, working from home. I'm an early riser and do my best work in the morning, so I could usually complete all of the work I needed to get done in a day by 1:00 p.m. or a little later. I'm sure you can see where this is going. You guessed it. Coffee and low-calorie snacks were used to tide me over during the morning, allowing a nice hunger to build that I would usually satisfy every day with a delicious, filling binge in the early afternoon. A nice drive around town, in the sanctity of my car, indulging my cheesy, greasy cravings. *Ahhh …* Then a quick purge when I got home. All up. All out. Check, check. Clean it up and it never even happened. *Ahhhh …* Then a nice solid workout with Guy after he got home and *\*voila!\** it was a perfect routine. I got my fix, no one knew, and I still looked fabulous. Yes, bulimics think like this. Yes, this is normal for us. And I might have continued like this for quite some time, many, many more years, if I hadn't hit that wall.

To this day, I'm thankful that it happened for me the way that it did. Even though I sat in the car and cried, bawled, wailed, and punched the steering wheel until my knuckles were soar. I finally had that moment. That overwhelming shame that saved me.

So, it was a normal day. I skipped breakfast. I had a salad and Diet Coke for lunch. It was around 1:30 p.m. and I was starving (because I was often, always, unconceivably starving), and Guy was at work for the rest of the day. I had my own car, and I had the time. I tried to stop myself by going on a fun, shopping errand first. Feed the craving with something else I hoped, but it gnawed at me in the store, clawed at me as I left the mall and walked past the outdoor tables of a little pizza joint and saw people eating huge slices of cheesy pizza. And I thought how unfair it was that those women could do that. Skinny little bitches could eat pizza and have stomachs that bunched like a bunny's nose when they bent over. Yes, my mind would sometimes take me all the way back to the beginning—to an old photo, to an old painful memory. Then I would decide: *"Fuck it. I'm doing it."*

I knew exactly where all the fast food places I liked to go were and I started my rounds. Because I had decided the particular Whataburger near our apartment was now off limits, my regular drive-thru regimen had changed a little to allow a trek uptown to a different Whataburger which also took me to a different Krystal and a different Taco Bell. Ones I did not go to quite as often, but it mattered none. That's the great thing about fast food chains. The food is the same shitty quality at every one of them.

So, I was halfway through my fix, three quarters of my patty melt down, dunking onion rings in a drunken delicious plunder, in my little gravy cup, and ordering at Krystal. (Yes, I could do all of this while driving. My knee is almost better than my hands at holding a steady line on the road.) My belly was pooched out. I had unbuttoned my pants, even unhitched and removed my bra, because it was more comfortable. And I had just taken a huge bite of patty melt that left a mayonaissy mess around my mouth when I saw it pop up on my phone. A text. From Guy.

"Where are you? Are you getting food?"

My heart thumping in my throat, the huge chewed-up wad of food just sitting in my mouth, I looked up, looked around. I wondered if Guy was, for whatever God-forsaken reason, near me in that part of town and had seen my car pass by. Perhaps he saw me in it. Maybe he saw me shoving a burger in my face. Then I saw it. *Fuck!* That Krystal, the one near the Whataburger on the *other* side of town was right across from a little Thai restaurant Guy and some of his partners went to on occasion. Where they would sit and eat lunch like normal people. The bench seats were positioned right near the windows that overlooked the Krystal drive-thru line. The restaurant windows were slightly tinted and I couldn't quite make out their faces, but I saw three suits sitting at a table.

In a panic, I tried to squint through the dark glass and I swore one face was turned towards me.

I flipped the fuck out. I peeled out of the drive-thru line, nearly missing the car in front of me. I skidded out onto the road, almost side-swiping an SUV with kids in the back. My tires squealed as I started driving as fast as I could away from there. I rolled down the window and started throwing my disgusting food wrappers and bags out. I wiped my disgusting face, made myself swallow the gross, fattening wad that was still in my mouth, and pulled over into a parking lot in tears. I wanted to go straight home and puke. Throw it all up and make myself another promise, that I knew even before I made it, I would not keep. But I thought, maybe if Guy knew, and maybe, just maybe, he wouldn't be so disgusted to the point he never wanted to see or talk to me again, maybe he could help me and I could finally get better. *"Maybe you should just tell him, Callie,"* for the first time my mind actually allowed this idea. With tears forming in my eyes and fear burning in my chest, I picked up my phone to text him back, my hands shaking with the horror of what I might have to say if he saw me, woofing down a burger in a fast food line.

"No, was just getting a coke while running errands." Then shaking, but knowing I had to ask it. I had to know.

"Did you see me?"

I could hear my blood pulsing behind my eyes while I waited for his response. Thump. Gush. Thump. Gush. Minutes went by. I was sweating because my body was overloaded with the work of trying to digest all the gross shit I had just filled it with. My stomach was starting to hurt because it was full, and this time I was just letting it sit. Finally, little circles popped up that indicated Guy was typing. It felt like the longest minute of my life before his words finally came through.

"Saw you? No. We just had a client stop by the office with a homemade Philippine dish. I thought if you hadn't eaten, you could come get some. It's so good. Lots of veggies!"

That's when I started crying! Screaming. Spitting. I was almost *not* relieved he hadn't seen me because I was almost ready to just admit to him that I was a broken person who needed help. That I was sick and I wanted to get better, I would get better, if he would just stay with me and help see me through. And I knew he loved me. So freaking much. Enough to think of me, even despite all my weird food stuff, and reach out to me because he knew I would love a healthy dish with "lots of veggies!" And I was the piece of shit who spent the afternoon shoving mountains of garbage into and puking vile piles of foul sludge *out of* the very mouth that would later kiss him. Guy. The man who loves me.

A part of me was angry he didn't yet know, because I didn't know if I had the courage to tell him anyway. I was scared that I might continue because he still didn't know. But, I couldn't go to his office and enjoy a nice dish with him and the other partners there that he works with because I was a fat fucking cow that could not be seen by anyone in my condition. My belly distended, my pants unbuttoned, my lipstick half cracked and eaten off, smears of ketchup still on my cheek. And I couldn't eat anything because my stomach was so full it was about to rip. Like seriously rip. *"That's what you should tell him!"* my demon whispered, taunting at me because he knew I wouldn't. He knew I was his. And, he was getting his biggest, heartiest laugh at me right now and I knew exactly what he wanted me to do.

And, I decided. Finally. Right then and there, I was not fucking doing it. Never a-fucking-gain.

*"You hear me! NEVER AGAIN!"* I screamed out loud in the car, spit hitting the wheel.

I could feel, in that moment, that something in me had changed. The thought that I was caught and the shame it instantly caused in me made me so embarrassed, so mortified, that I felt exceedingly worse than I did the moment this all started— when I saw a stupid picture of myself topless and thought I looked like a fat, chubby boy. Even if I did, it was nothing I had done to myself. It was nothing to be ashamed of. It was just the way my natural body looked, but it was healthy then. Not sick. I instantly saw in my mind all of the horrid things I had done to my poor body since that day. All of the times I stuffed her to the point of pain, then stuck my fingers down her throat and made her throw up, to the point of crying, shitting, peeing, bleeding.

I really did feel like two people—one that just wanted to be happy and healthy and could care less if that meant she would forever carry around ten extra pounds and Care Bear belly. Then there was another—a heinous, snarly bitch. A stick-thin, knobby-jointed, vile woman, her hair half falling out, her skin aged and grey, her teeth cracked and falling out. *She* was the one who was shoving a burger into my mouth and laughing. She was the one sticking her bony, slimy fingers down my throat and laughing. Pointing at my red, vomit-strewn, swollen face in the mirror when I finished, heartily cackling at me. To the point of tears. She was so ugly and sick and mean. She was also me. Had been for years. I was my own demon.

NO MORE.

I finally saw it all. The stupidity of it. The ridiculousness. The danger. While I didn't know just yet how I was going to fix it or what was going to happen if I started eating like a normal person, I knew I was going to do it. This was the end. This was the time to make that decision and hold to it: I AM STOPPING RIGHT NOW.

Yes, even with my binge just complete. Yes, even with a distended gut full of burger and onion rings that would make me fat. Even then. It was actually the perfect time. Because it was the moment when I had the strongest desire to punish my body, to get every last forbidden bite up, and get skinny again. That was that moment that I was going to stop. I was not going to throw up.

I would face whatever consequences came. I wiped the tears from my face. I buttoned my pants, painfully worked my bra back on under my nasty stained shirt and straightened up. I cleaned my face up, fixed my lipstick and texted Guy back: "Thanks honey. But I already ate. Enjoy it and bring some home to me! I can't wait to see you!" Boy was that true. I was not injured, going to the emergency room, permanently scarred or worse. I was alive and still seemingly healthy. And I still had Guy. And I had so much to look forward to. I was going to eat that "so good" Philippine dish later and I was going to keep it down and enjoy it, like a normal freaking person. Thinking it, this day, might be the beginning of the end of all it—my never-ending, exhausting battle with food—I was actually looking forward to it.

Painful as it was with my stretched-out tummy, I made myself go to the car wash and I spent an hour washing, cleaning and vacuuming my car. Never again was it going to be filled with the stench of corn dogs and chicken gravy. I went home, took off the clothes I was wearing and started a load of laundry along with the other dirty clothes. Never again were my garments going to come home with the scent and stains from a fast-food binge on them. Without looking at the toilet, without weighing myself, and without examining my body in the mirror (all things I used to do every time before I stepped into the shower), I spent an indulgent half hour washing, cleaning, shaving, and exfoliating myself from head to toe. Looking at my body for the first time in a completely different way. There she was, standing upright, able to walk, run, jump, fly. She was healthy and strong this whole time, ready to take me around the world on adventures and look what I had been doing to her. I shaved, clipped my nails. Pumiced my feet. Rubbed lotion everywhere. I blow-dried and curled my hair and put a little make-up on (things I rarely did in a normal work-from-home day). Then I went for a walk, not an intense workout-walk, just a dressed-up, out-on-the-town normal walk, outside in the sunshine, like normal healthy people do.

These were all things I did rarely in a normal day, but I did them all in an effort to show my body how sorry I was and how much better I was about to start treating her. I also dressed up nice, in actual going-out-on-the-town clothes, something I did rarely. Normal work days saw me working in PJ's until mid-morning, then I would switch to workout clothes, which offered both a quick, low maintenance get-ready routine, and the stretchy freedom to accommodate both my disgusting binge-and-purge routine followed by my way-too-rigorous workout routine. Instantly I realized how much easier it would be to refrain from indulging in the disgusting routine of stuffing myself and throwing it all up if I just dressed up and went out more often. All of a sudden, it wasn't an option because when you're with people and you're all tidied up, you don't even indulge the thought of it. A mayonnaise-smeared face and distended gut are not going to pair well with that outfit. Instantly, you just eat normal and have a normal day, because you're dressed for it, and imagine that, life is good. Not just good. Better. And so much freaking easier!

Amazingly, after I did all of that, just a few hours later my tummy had settled out. While I wasn't hungry again yet, that would be a few more hours still, I had forced it all to stay down. I had not thrown it up. I know that might seem like a small accomplishment to some of you, but for me that was huge. That was the first time I had binged and forbidden myself from throwing it up. There had been other times, sure, when I'd had a near-miss and had to unfortunately keep some of the bad stuff down, for longer than I would have liked, in order to hide my sickness. But, this was the first time I did it by choice. Even with a toilet right there. Even with the freedom and solitude to do it. Even with the secret still kept. That's what made the difference. I did it by choice.

Inside, I felt I had finally made that decision. Not just thought about it. Not said to myself, "I should" or "I will." But "I just did." I made that decision. And it all starts there. It all starts in your mind and with your decision to see your eating disorder for what it really is—a dangerous, disgusting, costly, and futile prison of your own making. Only then can you decide to stop.

And, I'm sure you're wondering if I told Guy that evening, over the Philippine dish? No. But I did start writing this book the next day and that's when the healing process began for me. I also kept the promise I made to myself that day. I have not thrown my food up since that moment. It's been almost six months now, and that's a huge accomplishment in the life of Callie. While I never dreamed as a young teenager, or even a young adult who struggled with food but who hadn't gone that far *yet,* that I would sink into such a sick, sad hole and keep myself there for so long, I can at least say I crawled out. And I'm hoping now I can be the voice that helps others, perhaps you, to crawl out, too.

Be the Callie I was that day.

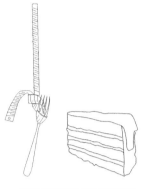

**CHAPTER FIFTEEN**

# THE END OF AN EATING DISORDER

Begins with THE DECISION TO STOP.

And not an "I should," or "I will," or "I need to stop." Not an "It would be nice if I stopped." But an "I'm stopping right now. That was the last time."

And, that's the easiest thing to say to yourself *while* you're indulging a food high. You're so happy then, you could promise to take up quilting and make one the size of Texas. You can promise anything then, because you're high and happy in that moment. You can also promise it right after you've purged. Because it's all out. You're skinny again. Clean slate. *"Where's that sewing machine?"*

The time when it's hard to make that promise is when you're hungry (because you haven't eaten in seven hours) and you're pacing the kitchen, peeking in the cabinets, trying to make yourself stop. You'll break any promise then. Or, imagine you've just eaten piles and mounds of whatever greasy, cheesy, sugary, calorie-laden stuff you like to put down in a binge and it's time to shuffle to the bathroom to take care of business. That's the moment you have to make the decision, promise yourself, and stop right then. Do not do it.

The current roar in your head—"Do it! Get it out! Throw up!"—will eventually subside. But hunger will come back. The craving will rise again, but you just have to be stronger. You have to get off the rollercoaster (starving then binging, starving then binging), put something normal and healthy in, and keep it down. I know it's scary. And I know it's embarrassing to even admit that—that eating normal food is scary. "Jesus, you're such a freak." But, you're not. Hundreds of thousands, even millions, of people feel just like you. It's okay. I've been there, done that. And, I almost cried after I ate my first plate of pasta and just let it sit. I could feel the satisfying lump in my stomach, I could still taste the oil and butter on my lips, and I was painfully aware of all of the fat, calories, and carbs that just went in. It was probably the first pasta dish I had consumed in a normal manner in fifteen years, and I was afraid of it. But, I was also resigned to stick with it. I had to harness my stubborn powers for good and use them to push myself toward healthy goals because I was tired of treating my body like a sewage plant.

So, I stuck with it. Pasta went down. Pork chops went down. Rice pilaf went down. Ratatouille went down. Jambalaya went down. And do you know what happened? It's the most amazing thing. My body started screaming, "My GOD, thank you! Thank *you! Thank you! Thank you!"* Then she started to look good. Then she started to *feel* good. I honestly can't believe I spent so many years hating and cursing food when it is so freaking good for me, and so good to eat. Even (and sometimes especially) the fats and carbs. Turns out many fats are very good for my hair, skin, and nails. And my boobs! My God, I had boobs again! *"Where've you been girls?"* And they would probably say, *"Hiding because you were a real bitch!"*

The very ironic, almost laughable thing about all of this, is that all the punishment and pain you're inflicting on yourself is an infinitely harder way to accomplish your end goal of looking and feeling good. Do you want to know the answer? The easiest, simplest solution to all of your hiding, and purging, the end of your exhausting, isolating, repulsive routine?

Just eat. Like a normal person. Eat with people. Eat normal amounts. Eat really good shit and your body will start to respond. She will start to heal. Her elasticity, her color, her sheen, her curves, and her strength will return. She will look the best she's ever looked as soon as you decide you are stronger than a sick addiction, and you are done disrespecting yourself.

Make that decision right now (*"Now dammit!"*) and go make a huge bowl of creamed spinach. Then curl up with a book and eat it! It's so good. So creamy. And so good for you!

Thankfully, I have a wonderful partner who loves to cook and is a fantastic chef. Guy makes amazing meals that I love to eat, not past the point of full, just until I'm satiated, happily satisfied, to where I feel fulfilled and fueled for hours. And, these meals make my body look and feel amazing. Without him, I'm not sure I would have been able to finally quit and build the healthy relationship I now have with food. I would like to hope so, but I'm just not sure. Had I continued to live alone, I may have continued on that terrible path. For years and years. But I look forward, now, to every meal we make and eat together (which is about 99% of them), and I have so much more time, energy (and money!) now to devote to exceedingly more important and rewarding things than catering to a debilitating food addiction.

And if you're thinking, "Well good for you Fancy Pants, but my life is harder, my addiction is stronger, my body will never look or feel the way I want it to, so it's not all cupcakes and sunshine for me. I can't just *decide* one day to stop and then it's done, it's over, I'm healed."

My response?

You're right. Only in that it will not immediately be done or over. You will not be immediately healed. It will take a long time, maybe months, maybe years, for you to finally re-wire your approach to food, to truly see weeks ahead where you know you will not binge or purge. It's going to take a lot of patience, commitment, and forgiveness from yourself. You have to be prepared to forgive yourself, because you are going to slip. You are going to struggle. It's going to be frustrating and embarrassing, because it is scary. But there is one area where you are wrong.

You can, right now, on this very page, decide to start on the path to recovery. You can make a commitment to yourself to change things, to start eating normal and see what happens. *Oh my God! Pasta?!* Yes, pasta! Occasionally pasta! I guarantee you will start to feel better, and you will start to feel incredibly silly that you spent so much time pursuing such a costly, dangerous, isolating addiction for so many years when the method to accomplishing what you were trying to obtain in the first place—to look and feel good—is SO MUCH EASIER.

Get this: You're supposed to eat three or four times a day. Snacks, too. You're also supposed to indulge occasionally in a nice serving of ice cream, cookies, cake. *"Whoa, really? Cake?"* Yes, really! Cake!

And, how about this: You should only work out three to five times a week, and thirty minutes is enough. That's enough! Any more is too much and you're depleting your body, forcing it to store fat for energy. Is any of this making sense? If you continue to binge and purge because you're not happy with the way your body looks, I can promise you, your disgusting routine is one of the primary reasons your body looks and feels like crap. You're making it worse. And, if you think you look phenomenal and that you can *only maintain that* through bulimia, again, I urge you to set up a camera in the bathroom and ask yourself: Do I look phenomenal there?

MAKE THAT DECISION.

Eating. Is. Good for you. It allows you more time to spend with people, doing things you enjoy. It frees up time and money so you can set and conquer new, exciting goals. You can build old relationships back and start new ones, this time with*out* your addiction in the way. Life is so much better on the other side. And if you're strong enough to stuff your fingers down your throat and heave and push and clench until you've ejected the entirety of your stomach contents out, I guarantee you're strong enough to beat this addiction. When you start to feel that craving for release, the high that you get when you start thinking about all the delicious foods you're about to eat, and that hungry *need* to shove something in your mouth and swallow, again, and again, and again, imagine yourself standing strong and tall, toe to toe with this addiction that has taken over and ruined your life. A monster standing right in front of you. What do you want to do? Curl down at its feet and start eating hand-to-mouth in front of the fridge like a coward? Fuck no!

Punch that Mother Fucker in the throat!

If you've truly decided you want to stop because you know this addiction is taking so much from you, that is what you'll want to do. And, I hope that is the image that will fill your mind when the cravings strike (because they will). Come up with a coping plan and implement it. Grab something small, filling, but healthy (a bottle of juice, a pack of nuts, fruit, a sandwich or something else) and *leave the house* to go do something you love to do. Go to the park for a walk. Go to the library and read a few chapters of an interesting book. Go see a movie. Hell, go to a trampoline jump zone place and just have fun for half an hour. In that moment, when the addiction is pulling at you, taunting you, making you think there is nothing that can bring you the same pleasure or release you feel you need at that moment, know that he is trying to win. Your demon wants to see you shoveling frosting into your mouth. He wants to see you hunched over the toilet, your gross slimy fingers gripping the bowl. He wants to see that defeated feeling you have afterward when your body feels exhausted and depleted, yet still fat and wanting more. If you go there, he wins. Time and again. Imagine him shaking his head, pointing at your many potty pictures on the wall, and laughing at you. I'm telling you: Shut it down.

Punch that beast in the throat and laugh at him.

*"I win this time, bitch!"*

It all begins with laughter. MAKE THAT DECISION.

Then find a friend you trust, who loves you, and tell him or her about it. Heck, do it over burgers. Because you can (and should!) eat. A burger.

Good things should go down.

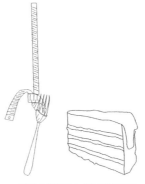

**CHAPTER SIXTEEN**

# THIS IS WHERE I LEAVE YOU: NOW YOU HAVE TO LET GO

So, I may have lied (just a little) when I told you it was easy. But it's not really a lie because that is true: maintaining a healthy weight and shape is ten thousand times easier to do the normal, nutritious way as opposed to the backwards what-goes-down-must-come-up way you and I have been doing it. The energy, time, and physical effort people who are anorexic or bulimic willingly devote to their eating disorder towers over the energy needed to maintain a truly healthy diet and exercise routine. So, physically, that is 100% true. It is so stinking easy. But, mentally—for you and for me—it will be anything but easy. The hardest part of all of this will be the mental accomplishment of finally letting go. Taking your white-knuckled fingers off (what you think are) the controls, because you're deathly afraid that is exactly what you will lose if you do. Control. Over your looks, your appearance, your personality, your path, your entire life. That's what will happen if you just kick back and let go.

Think that sounds crazy? How would you feel if I told you the first thing you need to do is sit down and eat a piece of cake? Yes, the whole slice. Yes, with frosting on it. Not just that little two-centimeter sliver you used to peel off with the edge of your fork and suck on that had less calories than a stick of gum. The whole slice. *"The whole slice? Frosting and all? Is she crazy?"* you're probably screaming to yourself. *"That's ridiculous. Cake's not even healthy. If I'm going to do this—eat. Normal. I'm at least going to do it the heathy way. I don't have to eat cake."*

You're right. You don't *have* to. I hate to break it to you, but if you're still *afraid* to eat a piece of cake, you have not yet let go. You've still got one clenched fist on the reigns, one foot entrenched on the other side of the line. And it may take a while (months, years perhaps) and many attempts at alternative coping mechanisms before you fully and finally let go of this disorder. It's just going to take time. Know that. It's also going to take some slips, some transgressions, some other weird habits you pick up because they at least help you stay—in the global scheme of things—tiptoeing toward the healthy side.

You may become a popcorn connoisseur. You may find you never leave home without a pack of Sour Patch candies. You may have an almost permanently red mouth from sucking on red Icee Pops. (That's actually not such a bad thing to often have— plump red-stained lips). You may take up knitting. Crosswords.

Raquetball. Jazzercise. Be thinking about things you've always wanted to try to do, because you're going to have some time on your hands and you'll need a (or perhaps many) seriously-distracting distractions.

Whatever your weird quirks become—as long as they are healthier habits than the ones you had before and they keep you progressing in the right direction—embrace them because it will be very difficult for you to let go of this obsession with food. The desire for it, the craving of it, the delicious, orgasmic over-consumption of it, then the pervasive, demonic, overwhelming need to somehow purge it, either with extreme, excessive exercise or by throwing it up. When you've had something consume such a huge part of every day for years, an addiction that filled the majority of your thoughts, letting go of that will cause a massive, nagging void. Trust me, I've been there. And while many things you take on in an attempt to fill that aching gap (activities, mental exercises, snacks, etc.) may be perfectly acceptable, smart, and healthy alternatives to bending and breaking your body to the will of your disorder, others may not. I can only hope with this monologue you are better prepared for the void and have a list of healthy things prepared to try to fill it. Things that do not include alcohol, drugs, random sex, random crime, pushing children or elderly people down and laughing at them. At the very least, I can save you this one by, yet again, sharing my stupid and embarrassing story. *You're welcome.* Whatever you do, don't become a Clencher.

Looking back on it, it's actually hilariously-ironic that in trying to get myself to mentally "let go," I made myself physically grip tighter than I ever have before. As I've mentioned, often people with long-standing eating disorders are Type A. The reason we foster and placate this disease for years is because we pride ourselves on how hard and far we can push ourselves, much harder and farther than others, much more than is healthy or necessary. This is why letting nature simply "take its course" and give us whatever natural body shape that was intended for us when our DNA first formed, without having any say, input, or control is infuriating. It pains and panics us to let go of the controls. Case in point: Callie the Clencher.

While deciding—that wretched, grease-smeared day in the parking lot—to never again cram my beautiful body full of disgusting grease, cheese, and gravy only to make myself throw it all up was an important first step, I (me, my meddling Mind) was, apparently, not ready to give up complete control. I did not yet believe that I could allow my body the egregious indulgence of normal, healthy meals without some tradeoff. *"Callie, Callie. Tssk, tssk. Your stupid, ugly body is not like that of other magically-perfect, happy people. If you eat normal stuff like a bagel, spaghetti, or a burger, you will instantly blow up. You'll get immediately fat and unhappy. Yes, immediately,"* my Mind would tell me. And, yes, I believed her. So, we made a deal, her and me. We decided that if Callie was going to be allowed to eat normal, she had to do something to earn it, something to burn off those evil, forbidden calories she just put in. Callie decided she would be allowed to eat normal, if and only if, she spent the entire day clenching some muscle group in her body. Man, that Callie. She's a smart one, I tell you.

And, knowing she had a monstrous gut, a huge hunk of muscle that filled the small, crunched space between her rib cage and pelvis, a Care Bear stomach, she decided to start with her stomach. This meant, the minute she woke up and started stumbling to the bathroom to brush her teeth and wash her face, her first thoughts were immediately to begin clenching her stomach muscles, only giving them a break upon exhaustion, at which time she picked up with a mad clenching of her thigh, ass, and back muscles, before she came back full circle to ab-clenching. Her thinking was that if these muscles are constantly flexed, surely she would be burning enough calories to compensate for the insane amounts of food her weak self was allowing to pass through her lips: toast for breakfast, a sandwich and apple for lunch (*Bread again? Holy crap!),* then pork and green beans for dinner. *What was she thinking? All of that normalcy is not allowed!* Your mind will continue to scream things like this at you. It will want to keep injecting itself, calculating and scolding you, even forcing you to do very stupid things to your body to try and compensate for the vast amounts of food you are putting in. *Normal amounts*, mind you.

I clenched for about a month solid, priding myself, even, on my ability to hold my muscles flexed for so long, while sitting so still that no one else noticed (other than the dribbles of sweat that leaked out from under my arms and behind my knees). This at first seemed to be something that allowed me to eat normal meals and dinners with less guilt and I believed I was just compensating in a somewhat normal way. I believed I could do that for the rest of my life. I'm lucky I didn't rupture more blood vessels and give myself spider veins all over, or a hernia. The problem with clenching all the time (every day for hours upon end, at least) is that your muscles never get a rest. They never get a chance to repair and rebuild. So, mine at least, starting to form into bulbous, squishy hunks of meat that were often so tired from all the clenching, they could barely clench anymore and they looked deceivingly like fat. After a month of it, I was two sizes bigger (three, depending on the pants) and squishier than ever. I looked like a body-builder who had fell off the wagon, bulky and bulbous.

Thankfully, I was in a strong enough mental place to choose the healthier of the two options I saw before me: 1) Reaching the conclusion that I had totally screwed up by allowing myself to eat normal—look where that had gotten me—and reverting in a violent slide back to the bowl; or 2) reaffirming my decision to finally kick this monster to the curb, and realizing that I had screwed up by reverting back to my old what-goes-in-must-come-out, unsuccessful, unhealthy ways and that the solution here was not to hug my salivating monster, grab his hand and flee to a pile of cake and grease in the corner. Rather, the solution was to let go. Just let go. Stop clenching. Stop counting. Stop scolding. Stop inserting myself there, at the control panel of my food intake and exercise regimen. Step back. Shut up and just follow a healthy plan, mindlessly.

The minute I stopped clenching, within days, my sore, tired, once-again-abused muscles began to thank me. They relaxed and bulged less. It was exactly what I needed: to feel I looked my very worst (swollen, fat, and squishy) and yet, in the face of that, to continue feeding my body nutritious, appropriately-sized servings anyway. It's like asking a gambling addict—when they have the time and money to do it—*not to gamble*. Rather, walk right by the dog track every day on the way home and just whistle as you pass it by. I had every reason to revert, blaming it on a flawed attempt that obviously did not work. *"See?! You see! I told you your body is not normal and that if you ate normal this would happen,"* I could have let my Mind convince me, easily. That would have been the easy thing to do. Then revert back. But I'm glad to say I didn't. Honestly, I didn't; because in my mind, I saw myself in the car with swaths of grease and ketchup on my cheeks, my pants unbuttoned to allow my bulging gut to pop out, my hands clenching a greasy burger and onion rings *then saying,* "You see! It's so easy!" as I shoved the burger back into my face and began chewing and fervently nodding. Thankfully, that image stopped me. *That* image kept me on track. I never wanted to be that sick, shameful person again. I never wanted Guy to see that person and if I stayed on track, he would not. That was one thing I could and was allowed to control. So I did.

When you are first starting the healing process and your body is going through many, many changes trying to adapt to, understand, and trust this new consistent, healthy stream of food you are providing it (not the previous plan where you would give and snatch back, deprive then gorge), she is likely going to show some changes. Maybe you will put on weight initially. Maybe you needed to. Maybe your muscles have atrophied and it will take time for them to rebuild and re-sculpt. All I can say is thankfully, my brick-wall moment was strong enough to keep my mental focus clear, even while my body was going through a bit of a frightening amorphous phase. Despite it, I was going to get better. I was going to eat normal. I wasn't going to be ashamed of myself or my eating habits anymore.

Once you have decided that and you have committed to eating normal, just give your body a freaking break. She's undoubtedly earned it. Don't weigh her and pinch her every day. Don't stand in front of the mirror, suck in, turn to the side, flex, whatever things you use to do when you were daily scrutinizing her. She's been through hell and back. Just give her a damn break. If she gets a little weird for a while, let it slide. Follow your routine. Tell your messed-up mind to shut up and butt out, and try to find something different, something more productive to do with all of that inner angst, anger, and fear. Thankfully—and I am not in any way ashamed to say that I am incredibly proud of myself in that moment when I finally stood before the mirror and *let go*. I stopped clenching. I stopped clinging so damn hard to something that was not good for me and did not work anyway. And I truly believe, in that moment, I stopped hating my body. I wasn't really happy with her, but for the first time I felt sorry for her. Yes, like she is some different person than me. I can only say that's how I honestly felt. But in that moment—when I finally decided to cut her some slack and stop staring over her shoulder all the time, picking at and commenting on her food, pinching her squishy parts, and basically making her feel like shit—I found my alternative coping mechanism:

Writing.

The minute all of these things poured into my head—the two Me's, my Mind and my Body, the entirety of my disease and how it had progressed, how at times it was disgusting and hard to look at, and how, at others, I could honestly laugh at it (*"You literally ate butter spray until you were Oompa Loompa orange. Really, Callie?"*)—I knew the first thing I wanted to do, *had* to do, was write all of these things down. Get them out. Let all of this toxic stuff pour out of me, so it would *be* just that: out of me. I actually *wanted* to share my story. I wanted to tell people how insanely and hilariously stupid I was, because it proved how lucky I was to still be here, with an intact gut and the throat of a songbird, even *capable* of talking. I was so goddam lucky, because I was finally able to see it all. The laughable futility of it, and—despite that, despite years of hard-core, in-your-face proof of that—my laughable, unwavering commitment to it. I was Sisyphus. And I was done. I wanted to tell my story to every other person out there who was bulimic, or who was even on the path to bulimia, or who knew, loved, and perhaps had spent years trying to help someone with an eating disorder or who was bulimic. I felt I had a story that could help them. My story.

So, I started writing. Feverishly writing.

That became my coping mechanism. Well, that and popcorn. I ate a ton of popcorn while writing this book, probably as many kernels as words. I'm not kidding. Sometimes four bags a day. But, those measly calories couldn't begin to compare to what I used to put down at my Whataburger stop during my drive-thru days (not to mention Krystal and Taco Bell, sometimes Krispy Kreme, after that). So, I forgave myself the excessive shoveling of food into my mouth that seemed necessary to quiet the mind-consuming need to remain skinny, because I was at least doing it in a healthier way. I wrote chapter upon chapter of this book, as I downed bag upon bag of popcorn. And one very good thing to come out of all my mad, bottled-up clenching was posture. I did learn to try to focus as often as possible on holding my core in and holding my frame up in a dignified manner. Is that a very simple, miniscule thing? Yes, but with immensely-rewarding consequences in my book (no pun intended), because it honestly makes me feel taller, slimmer, and more proud of myself. Whatever healthy coping mechanism gets you through, embrace it.

Because this—the paralyzing thought of letting go and knowing you (your wicked, washed-up mind) is no longer allowed to control your diet and exercise regimen—will be the hardest, most infuriating part. Find a suitable diet and exercise program that you like. Anything that recommends moderate, healthy intake and moderate, healthy exercise. I've included my favorite in the next "Tips and Resources" chapter. Follow it and tell your meddling mind to shut the heck up. When she whispers to you how many fat grams are in the yolk of an egg—*"Oh my God, you ate the yellow part!?"*—you tell her to shut up. When she tries to convince you to do fifty more crunches or two minutes more than the workout recommends—*"Keep pushing yourself, you wimp!"*—you tell her to shut up. When you've just eaten a healthy, filling meal with friends, followed by a small slice of cake and she starts massaging the saliva glands in your mouth, hoping you'll sneak out of the room to go throw up—*"You know you want to. That cake is right now turning to fat."*—you tell her: SHUT UP.

I often had to close my eyes and literally say this to myself. Not only to quiet the voice, but also to remind myself what the voice was saying. It was encouraging me to try to sneak back in there, grab a little bit of control, and make myself do something unhealthy. The impulse is so strong initially, I often did not even perceive it as my own internal voice, making me feel bad about doing something good for my body, about eating and working out in a normal, healthy way. I would often find—after eating a nutritious filling meal or finishing a moderate workout—that I had this bad feeling, like a tinge of anger that I wasn't pushing myself harder, that I was somehow being lazy. And it wasn't until I would shut my eyes and whisper "shut up" to myself that the feeling would finally shake free and I would once again feel good about myself. I literally needed to be reminded that was my old, sick self, trying to inflict her wrath. And, she's so good at it, she's so seductive and stealthy, that I often didn't realize it was her who was making me feel guilty and lazy. I am anything but lazy. "I don't feel guilty. I'm no longer ashamed," I would say out-loud. "I am making my body strong and beautiful and healthy," I would tell myself (often in the mirror). And I would often then point a finger at the mirror and sneer: "And you! You little bitch! How did you get back in there? Shut up and go away!" This would also often induce a very satisfying laughing fit when I would realize: *"Yes, Callie, you are talking to yourself in the mirror."* But I knew I was not crazy. I was just healing. And laughter is a huge part of it.

One last thing I must do before I bid you farewell, tell you "This is where I leave you," and say I hope, beyond every aching impulse you have to over-eat, over-exercise, over-anything, that my words and images somehow sneak in, my story somehow gets through and helps you stay strong. When your mind starts to whisper and claw at you, imagine me in my final drive-thru moment, bloated, grease-streaked, and stuffing my already-full mouth trying also to convince you. "Of course you should do it! Binge! Indulge!" I say, while pushing one pink wad of half-chewed food aside with my tongue before biting the head off a cheese burrito. "This is a super-attractive, upstanding, healthy way to carry yourself. You're going to look and feel great. Here, want some cheese sauce?"

I hope that, in the slightest way, works for you. But before I leave you with that, I'm sure you are wondering whether I finally bucked up and told Guy all of this. Because, if you, too, are feeling that you are finally going to do this—stop wrecking yourself, stop being ashamed, and finally get healthy—you know the first thing that makes you *not* want to do that is the thought of telling someone. Or better yet, telling *your* someone. Your person. But you know you have to tell someone. Either, because: a) you're wise enough to know, if left to your own deceitful, crafty devices, you'll likely find a way to convince yourself to go back there, revert back to your old bad habits; or b) I'm telling you: if left to your own deceitful, crafty devices, you will find a way to convince yourself to go back there, revert back to your old bad habits. Not telling someone about your heroic and very hard decision to get better and start the healing process is like a drug addict saying they're going to quit, but refusing to flush the goods down the toilet. They're not truly committed.

Telling someone about your eating disorder is like shining a blazing light on all the dark corners where you used to go and do that. It flushes them out and makes it very difficult to go back to your hiding spot and sneak your stash. You will now be discouraged to do it because you know the person you've told will be disappointed in you and hurt by your failure. That layer of accountability is a must because you cannot hold yourself accountable. You just can't. You're too sick to be trusted with that role. You have to tell. And it may stand as the reason that you do not, for years, put an end to your eating disorder and decide to finally get better, because you are afraid and ashamed to tell. I 100% get that. I was that. I did that.

But I also told Guy. Not immediately. *Are you crazy?* Not after my Whataburger break-down. Not after I decided to start clenching. But, boy I wish I had then. It would have saved me a hard month of clench time and another, even harder, two months, of squishy, angry recovery. Not even when I started writing this book. But, I did tell him when I finished. When I believed it could actually be a book. Not just an article. Not an essay. Not just some story I wrote for my own benefit. But a no-shit serious book that might genuinely help some people, perhaps hundreds of people. Maybe thousands of people! That finally gave me the strength I felt I needed to tell him. And, I wanted to tell him. Over the years, Guy and I have shared a lot—a lot of hurt, a lot of joy, several lost loved ones, lost friends, lost opportunities, tough economic blows, and even tougher career changes. We were as close as I believe any two people can be, and I felt like my eating disorder was the last secret I had been holding back from him. I was also proud of my decision to quit, my fortitude to see it through, and my bravery in deciding to share my story, and I knew he would see that, too.

But I wasn't telling myself the typical clichés. It's funny, when you hear other people share their story about overcoming an addiction, and they always say whoever you are afraid to tell is going to be supportive. "They're going to be so proud of you for quitting. They're going to love you no matter what. They're going to be so grateful you finally told them so they can help you." While all of that is true, you already know all of that. Honestly, you do. People who truly love you are going to see a sickness you endured as just that—a sickness that you are recovering from—not something that in any way even sparks the idea, much less convinces them, to flat-out leave your side. They may be a little freaked out, a little unsure of exactly why you felt the need to do this to yourself and how best to talk to you about it. You, the put-together, capable, confident person they likely see you as (because that's likely the very persona you daily embody and convey: professionalism, success, and poise). But, they will not leave your side. And, if you were like me, you know that, but, that's not what you truly fear. Desertion?

No, you are afraid they will see you as less and they will love (desire, crave, want, share with, touch, kiss, talk to, insert your fear here) you less. You fear that after you tell them, they will see you differently—as someone who is a little unstable, a little (or perhaps very) gross, a little (or perhaps very) fucked-up in the mind. My biggest fear was not a straight-out abandonment by Guy, but the slightest pulling away. An instinctive desire that he would experience, after I told him, to disconnect just a little or distance himself from me because, once he learns the terrible, inexcusable, totally-demented things I had been doing to myself for decades, he would not want to remain as closely-connected to me. I was deathly afraid of that slight head tilt, that letting go of my hand, an inner cringe I would see in his eyes when I told him about my eating disorder that would change us forever, no matter how many times he would say, "I'm here for you, I'm proud of you, I support you." Blah, blah, blah. While we, bulimics, do need all of those things, we are still very strong-willed, controlling people who don't like to *need* anything. Meaning, those commonplace support-group type answers aren't going to give us the confidence and comfort to assure us that the person we tell will not, even in the slightest, change their mind about us.

By leaning on Guy in this way and revealing something about myself so huge and deep and fucked-up and freaky, I was deathly afraid I would ruin us. That was my biggest fear. But, more than that, I feared a relapse. I feared a life of puking and hiding, vomiting and crying, binging and lying. I was sure I couldn't maintain a life like that anyway and keep Guy and I as close as we were, a direction I knew was only growing closer and more awesome by the day, and leaving less and less room for my stupid, unnecessary eating disorder. And I was grateful for that. I felt I finally had a shot here to choose the right path. Finally! I had been at crossroads like this before and because I wasn't in a very good place at those times (I was worried about law school, I was angry in my marriage, I was stressed about my job, etc.), I made poor choices. I turned left and dug a deeper hole for me and my disease. But this time, self-employed with my career in much better balance and control, and living happily with a man who was exciting, funny, healthy, and who offered me a fantastic, story-filled rich life of travel and adventure, I felt I owed it to myself—and to him—to try. I had to take a leap of faith and trust Guy with this huge, scary thing. I had to. If Guy and I were going to build an honest future together, it had to stand on the past, and I was proud of the person I was becoming.

I had to tell him. I was going to tell him. And, I was even surprised at myself for deciding to tell him. *Callie, are you crazy?* "Yes, apparently, but here goes," I responded back, while driving to meet him to do it. It was the morning after I had just completed my first complete draft of this book, and I knew I was going to do it. Then or never.

And I did it! I told him! Not just that I had been a "tad bulimic in the past," before I met him. But that I had been bulimic recently, while with him, while living with him, on the same days I ate dinner with, kissed and slept with him. I had been bulimic right under his nose, right behind the bathroom door, and hiding it from him. Man, that was some really hard shit to get out.

And, it was sloppy and awkward, anything but eloquent, and probably one of the most embarrassing moments in Callie history because I was so apologetic and childlike, snot-nosed and sniffling, nothing remotely like the strong, witty voice you hear here. And I can't really tell you why. Guy just cripples me because, with him, I am totally exposed. I am totally vulnerable because he holds my very happiness and I know it. Guy is woven into my self-confidence and, if anything threatens to compromise our trust and connection in the slightest, I just fall apart. I start bumbling and crying and lose the ability to form complete sentences. It just is what it is. I think I heard it best in a lyric: "What I can sing at the top of my lungs on a stage to a crowd, I can't bear the thought of telling you out loud." I know I looked and sounded like a scared child that day at lunch. But that is exactly why I chose to tell him at a restaurant, in public, where I couldn't go completely berserk and on a day when I knew he would have to get back to the office afterward so I wouldn't have this "You're sick and weird" spotlight on me for hours afterward. I could be alone for a while to regroup, then make him a fabulous dinner that evening (because I could cook then), and fuck his brains out and everything would be normal.

And I did. And it pretty much was. Guy is not a man of big, sappy words (which I am quite fond of actually), but he is my person, my rock. And, he told me later that evening (after the exquisite fuck I might add): "All I care about is you. That you're healthy and happy and you're in my life. Nothing else matters." That was the extent of the conversation we had about it, and I hope it will remain that way. While I did not share every disgusting detail with him that I have shared here (you're welcome), it was because I knew his first reaction, when I told him I had written a book, would be to ask to read my book. He would learn all the disgusting things then. The important thing was that I told Guy the truth, *i.e.*, not that I had just been "a tad bulimic" before I met him, but that I had been a raging bulimic for years, even while I was with him, even while I was living with him. That was the hard thing to say, but I was also thankful after that snotty speech, that I could also straighten up and tell him: "I'm healing now. I'm getting better. I haven't done *that* and I have eaten healthy and normal for three months now. Three months! The longest since I was a teenager. I am through with all of that. I am better than all of that." I'm confident I sounded quite adult- and Callie-like, strong and vibrant, when I told Guy those things.

And, while the thought of him reading this book paralyzed me, it also made me (as Guy always does because he believes in me) make this manuscript better. It made me take the time to imagine him reading it, which forced me to craft it with a keener, more patient artist's eye. And I knew that when I felt it was finally perfect enough for his supportive blue eyes, I would let him read it. Guy has read everything I've ever written. Guy is often the first person to read anything I write. He is the person who inspired me to start writing and he is the reason I am now a self-employed writer and world-traveler to boot.

Guy, when you read this, know how much more of a person I am because I went through all of this shit and clawed myself through to the other side. Everything this wondrous world has to offer, I know we will go seek it out. We will pursue, see, hear, try (and now taste!) all of the amazing things that await us in our marvelous future together. And, if any part of this grosses you out just a little (or maybe a lot), promise me you'll remember all the mind-blowing blow jobs, forget and forgive my past, and know how impossibly-much I love you. You are the reason I am so many things today—well-traveled, happy, healthy, excited about my amazing future, and feeling so, so lucky to live the life that I do.

I am the reason, too. While I'm not sure why I made all of those bad decisions so many years ago—why I decided to let one semi-bad food habit grow to such weird Oompa-Loompa lengths, until the decision to make myself throw up was okay, and then it was not only okay, it was bliss and then it was not only bliss, it was a horrible, seemingly-unshakable addiction—I know that I did break it. I kicked that bastard in the throat and I am an infinitely stronger person for it. The things you do and choose and conquer make you who you are, your mind and body as one, and you just have to embrace, learn from, and build on them. And tell the people you love about them. Share your story.

I hope my story impacts you, that is the reason I told it. And it is the reason you should tell yours too. Telling drags your snarling, nasty monster-of-a-disease out into the blaring daylight, into the town square stocks so you can no longer hide and binge with him in a shameful corner. Once he's out in the open, withering and rotting under the harsh stares of those who love you, you'll find you have less desire to go sit next to him while your friends, family, and guy watch, shoveling cake into your face. Telling will lessen your desire to do it because it will make you accountable. And the best news? Telling will guarantee that you never have to have that overwhelming, heart-pounding feeling of panic you often get when you think you may have been caught, because there will be no more opportunity to "catch you." Telling will eradicate the fear you have been fighting for years over that huge, panic-stricken "I've been discovered" moment.

The people you love will know you *used to* do that but that you've made the very brave decision to stand up to your addiction and work very hard toward the goal of getting better. Telling is like stealing your monster's thunder. It weakens his hold. And, trust me, your "guy" (be it a guy or girl or anything in between) will be grateful you told him so he can help you heal and experience the reward of life with a healthier, happier you. Decide to do it, pick a time, and get ready for some snotty sniffles, because it's not going to look or sound pretty. But once you do it, it's done. And after that—once all of the hiding and shame and fear of being discovered and deserted, because that's not what will happen—is complete, the rest is gravy. (To be had with turkey at Thanksgiving, like normal folk, not poured over a pile of greasy onion rings, like drive-thru Callie. You're so much better than that.)

But with that last nugget, I have to leave you to it. My story is now told. My journey shared, so hopefully you can follow a similar path to being a badass who beats your eating disorder, too. You'll come out a much stronger person on the other end, I promise. Hopefully with a strong, new humorous perspective on the whole debacle and a newfound appreciation for your ability to give an exceptionally mind-blowing blowjob. *Cheers to you my recovering friend!*

If you haven't had that brick-wall moment yet, one is coming. When all of your shame and fear culminate in a heart-thumping moment of sheer panic. And you will wish in that moment, you were anyone but your sick, sordid self. Who wants to experience that? Why not beat it to the punch and save yourself the painful, unnecessary a-fibs. Let this book be your brick-wall moment. Why not? Make the decision to stop. Right now. Then, commence the easy stuff: the physical.

I've included a couple of tips and resources in the next chapter that helped me, but the physical part is really rather easy. This is not rocket science. You know what needs to be done. Rid your current life, cabinets, fridge, and living situation of the opportunity to binge and purge (either in the form or throwing up or exercise). Throw away all of your old binge food. Go buy raw carrots, broccoli, lettuce, chicken, pork, bread, rice, potatoes—normal shit that you have to cook before you can down it whole. Take the lock off of the bathroom door. Find friends or a fitness group to workout with. Then pick a healthy, balanced diet and exercise program to follow (which ensures you are now eating and working out like a normal, healthy person). Then you'll probably need to pick up some new, weird underwater basket-weaving habits to help keep you on this track (because your mind will want to force you to eat or workout in any way that does not mimic that of a normal, healthy person). And, give your blessed body a break. From the mirror, the scale, and your daily ridicule while you start eating normal. That's the easy "check, check, check" work-your-way-down-the-list stuff.

Then? After all of those really hard steps, comes the hardest of all. That's right, it gets harder. The physical stuff is tea time at Day Camp compared to the Death March that lies ahead in conquering the mental side of this disease. And it is the reason I give it only a grazing pass in this book, while spending the rest of this monologue trying to give you every weapon I can think of—clubs, chains, metaphors, images, me too's—to help you beat the real beast: your sneering, domineering, addicted mind.

And, yes, you can thank only yourself for creating this vicious monster that will test you to the absolute lengths of your rod-iron will power and strength of character. Your monster is mean and cruel and wants only to punish you because she is so, so angry. She's mad her body does not look and feel the way she wants it to. She is infuriated that she cannot control the things that happen in her life—whether she will be successful, happy, pretty, loved, hurt, rejected—by controlling your food intake and output with a vicious whip and fist. She is one pissed-off, snarly bitch and she's not going to just saunter away without a fight. She's you. He's you. And, shutting your own inner tormentor down will be the hardest thing you have to do. It will take the longest. It will cause you to falter. It will drag you to the mirror in tears, trying to slip its fingers back into your neck, break your will, and bend you back down in front of the toilet. Do not let it.

Tell your wicked mind to shut up, stop counting and calculating, stop picking on and punishing you, stop with the in-and-out. Unfortunately, this is where I must leave you, at the hardest part, but hopefully with every humorous weapon and image I could afford you to beat it.

Stop clenching. And just let go.

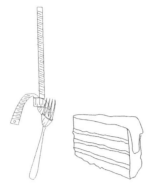

# TIPS ON RECOVERY AND RESOURCES

While I can share plenty of tips and tricks that helped me stick with the decision to let go, and I hope they help you, it is the actual decision that is the hard part; and that's what this book is intended to ignite in you. After that, any modest, reasonable healthy diet and exercise regimen will do. And, because you are so disciplined, you are so Type A and so driven, you'll find becoming healthy ridiculously easy. You will likely feel embarrassed by the many, many hours you spent previously trying to accomplish what is actually so very easy. But, you have to forgive yourself for it. Simply vow to use the newly-acquired free time ahead in healthy, rewarding ways, thanking your lucky stars every day that your throat is still intact.

You can now begin to enjoy your life more and bring more people you love, and who love you, in. You will no longer have to spend an hour (or more) each day locked inside, curled up in a pile of packaged foods and Tupperware tubs, so you can eat alone. You'll be able to go out to lunch with colleagues, enjoy a nice dinner on the town with friends, cook for family when they come over, then actually sit around the table and appreciate a nice meal with them. Eating will be something you look forward to and enjoy sharing with people you love. And get this: You will grow the number of people in your life that you love. With all of that time you used to spend stupidly binging alone now freed up, you can go out for nice meals with people, or take a new class at the gym, join a dance studio, go to concerts, or a thousand other things that I can assure you will bring you more pleasure than binging and will cause no guilt or pain.

In the meantime, while you're healing, and struggling, and questioning whether everything in your life is going to crumple because you're (*"Oh my God!"*) *eeeaating*—trust me, it will not—I want to share a few tips and tricks that helped me along the road to recovery. I hope they can help you, too:

**Posing.** Before you can ever start to see your body as one that is always, 100% of the time, beautiful, you have to realize the perfectly-arched, smooth-tummied, separated-thighs images you are trying to live up to are what those people look like when they're posing. You probably look just as sexy (*if not MORE sexy!*) when you pose and are photographed from a flattering angle. How often is this—5% of the time? Versus the other 95% when you're likely sitting slouched, your tummy pooched out, your thighs touching (*"Say it ain't so!"*). Yet, you (sick and twisted You) will likely stand in front of your mirror in the harsh light of your bathroom, let your body slouch to unflattering angles, then compare yourself to Rosey Posey. These women, men, models, etc. are posing. They are sucking in. They are arching their backs. They are popping their hips out to create flattering angles. *They do not look like that when they are standing in front of their own mirrors at home*. They look just as bad as you think you do when you're slouching. Don't believe me? Take this in: http://www.health.com/fitness/body-positive-before-and-after-photos. And then *stop* the torturous, inaccurate comparison you keep forcing on yourself.

**Posture.** Sound silly? It's really not. I'll bet one of the main reasons you hate how you looked in that awful photograph (that perhaps changed your life for decades) is because you didn't have good posture in that picture. You were slumped over, which makes your huge belly rolls bubble out, or maybe your tummy even tumbles out and sits on your thighs. Mine does, when I don't have good posture. Imagine yourself as one of the highfalutin, dainty ladies from the 1800s in their big bouffant hoop skirts, their bodies standing straight aloft, their waists cinched in girdles. Imagine it, then try to replicate it, only without the torturous undergarments. Holding your back up and aligned, bringing your shoulders back and pulling your core in makes you look and feel taller and thinner. Another bonus, it makes your boobs or pecs look bigger. *Fantastic!* You also give off the impression that you are put together, respectful, and strong in character. I'm not kidding. You think it's crazy, but try it for a day. Especially when you're eating, holding your body upright will give you a much sharper indication as to when you're appropriately full, and focusing on posture will also take your mind off food. Holding good posture is also very good for your shoulders, your back, and your core muscles. Win-win! And, as if you needed any more persuading, Bonus Point Number 253: Maintaining good posture will ensure you look more like that "posing" version of yourself more of the time. *"Snap that photo anytime. I'm always ready!"*

**Popcorn.** Call it the three "P's" if you'd like: Posing, Posture and Popcorn. Whatever helps you remember these tips, cut yourself some damn slack, and stay on track—that is the goal. One of my ultimate weapons against that rumbling, growing, roaring craving to binge, to allow myself that satisfying release, was popcorn. As I mentioned before, one of the best things to do when the craving hits is to eat something small and healthy and get immediately, vividly in the public eye. Leave the protection of home and go to a public place (library, park, grocery store, shopping mall, movie theatre, etc.) and do something fun and pleasurable that both distracts you and—because you're in public (not a very convenient place to go on a filthy, embarrassing binge)—keeps you accountable. But, I am also very aware that bulimics are usually incredibly busy people. You do not think you can spare the time to try and get healthy, to buy organic, raw foods, learn how to cook them, make healthy meals, or workout on a regular basis to keep whatever you eat off. Ironically, however, you will always make time for that hour you need to binge and get that necessary "release" that allows you to get your mind reset and get back on the highly-stressful hamster wheel that is your daily life—or so you think.

The great thing about popcorn is that (whether you make it from scratch by heating kernels or opt for the "smart pop" quick-and-easy microwave version) it is cheap, easy to stock, and lasts a while. It is also easy and quick to make, very low calorie and healthy, *and* can be eaten very slowly. One of the most pleasurable, satisfying elements of a binge is the repeated placement of food into our mouths. The flavor, the satisfaction of swallowing it down. You can do this slowly with popcorn for an hour or more—make two bags back to back if you need to. That's like 300 calories, maybe, and very little fat—and get that hand-to-mouth "fix" without going *there*, without doing *that*. This is like chewing gum for the smoker who is trying to quit. It will help pass the hours until it is time for you to eat a regular meal again. And if you're busy working, you can probably eat popcorn and keep at it, at least I could with primarily an office job. But, any kind of candies, nuts, little bags of trail mix, etc. can serve the same purpose. Something you can slowly eat or suck on to satisfy a bit of that "eat" craving that's roaring in your head, give you a little sustenance in case you really are hungry (sometimes it's hard to tell the difference when you've been re-wired for so long), and get you past that moment and to the next mealtime in a healthy way. It may sound silly. I care none. Popcorn often saved me many, *many* a trip to the vomit room when I was recovering. If it can do that, there's nothing silly about it. Humor me. Just give it a try.

**Peace.** Let's add one more "P." Peace. You have to make peace with food. You have to learn, and program your brain to understand: *your body needs food.* Food is not the enemy. It can be your very best friend. It can and should be enjoyed, shared, occasionally indulged, and can become the healthy centerpiece of your new life. I am shocked at how much I *enjoy* cooking now. When I don't have plans to eat out, Guy and I have plans almost every night too cook an amazing meal together, and I love not only eating it, but making it. The way the garlic sizzles in hot oil, the way it makes the kitchen smell like a warm Italian restaurant, the way the flavor of the dish grows and enhances as it simmers, sautées, or reduces down. I believe you will find cooking is an infinitely better pastime than eating ice cream out of your big Tupperware bowl.

And, it is not only pleasurable but necessary. Your body needs fuel; it needs steak and chicken and rice and bread and a wealth of deliciously-satisfying fruits and vegetables. It needs these to build beautiful muscles, fill out your natural curves and provide strength and depth to the areas of your body around your stomach in order to pull it in as your new lean core. The only way you will ever fix yourself and slaughter that demon in your mind is if you make peace with food. The answer is to eat! Several times a day. Often with people you love to be around. And you need to eat many good (and, in addition to healthy, I mean delicious, satisfying, better-than-sex) foods. That's the solution. Eat delicious, healthy food. I mean, how bad does that sound. Really?

I focus on these particular tips because they are primarily a response to what is happening in your mind. You have to start there because that's where an eating disorder begins. That's where you initially plant that seed and then start to nurture it, until it grows out of control, like a black, gnarly vine that twists and grips any thought in your mind relating to food. So, that is the area you will have to focus on first—your mind. It is also the area that will give you the most trouble because the roots are so deep, the fear is so big, and that snarly demon is so damn loud. But, you must start with your mind and your relationship with food. Begin to make peace there and the rest will come so easily. At least compared to the discipline required for what you have been doing. Getting better feels like finally letting go, of a knotted rope that you've been squeezing for years, your muscles exhausted and your hands calloused and blistered from it. Mentally, all you have to do now is just let go.

**FitnessBlender**

After that, a healthy lifestyle is really a no-brainer. You just eat healthy foods in moderation and workout in moderation. Personally, I like www.FitnessBlender.com because there are no gimmicks and it's a scientifically-backed, proven healthy routine that is EASY TO DO. I also connected with this platform early on because the wife and co-founder, Kelli, who is a beautiful, strong, inspiring woman, bravely put a video testimonial together documenting her own battle with and recovery from an eating disorder. This was one of the first times I ever saw someone talk about anorexia, exercise bulimia, binge-eating, and full-blown bulimia on a public platform. It was a powerful moment for me and influential in my choosing to share my story here. You can watch Kelli's courageous disclosure and motivational story here: https://youtu.be/VM99CXSPcVM

Once you begin to heal, forgive, and re-train your mind (which may take years), the remainder is simple and easy. You should eat three meals a day and snacks. You should eat mostly healthy but also indulge occasionally. And you should workout or do something active three to five times a week. That's it. That's the big magic secret you thought was so unattainable. But, it will remain unattainable for you, until you realize three things:

1. What a heathy you looks like.
2. What a healthy you will never look like (which may be a mental image that likely only 2% of the people in the world look like; and it's even more likely many of those people don't look like that in reality because they are posing in a photo-shoot, or, if they do, they are unhealthy and sick).
3. What striving to look like those people turns you into.

Beyond that, just follow any basic diet and exercise regimen that focuses on balance and moderation: healthy meals, healthy portions, healthy workouts. Any one of them will be infinitely easier to follow than: starve all morning, go on a monster binge every afternoon or evening, then puke it all up and eat nothing until tomorrow. Oh, and live alone, shun people, turn down any invitation that might involve food, yellow your fingers, risk your entire gastro-intestinal system, stick your fingers down your throat every day, and splash vomit on your face as you puke. Seriously, which sounds easier, Sisyphus?

One last thought:

**About Those Numbers on the Scale**

I really don't believe people recovering (or who have recovered) from an eating disorder who say, "I never look at the numbers on the scale anymore." Bullshit, yes you do! I do, however, believe those who say, "Okay, I do look, every day, probably a couple of times a day, but the number doesn't bother me as much now. Whether it's up a little or down a little, it doesn't have as much of an impact and I don't react violently to it the way I used to." That sounds like the truth.

Most people who are trying to recover from an eating disorder and be healthy (as well as many perfectly normal, healthy people who have not yet, and I hope never will, develop an eating disorder) look at a scale once or twice a day, mainly to see if they are *maintaining*. That's what I do now. Having been on a weight loss-and-gain roller coaster for decades, I have seen my weight fluctuate from an alarming 118 to an oversized 172 and everything in between. Once I finally stepped (or jumped, rather) off the roller coaster, started eating healthy, normal meals, and started working out in healthy, normal doses (oh, and after the bulbous Callie the Clencher weight finally settled out), I have found 145 to 150 pounds is a good weight for me. And, yes, I often have many people, when I tell them that number, respond with "No, you're not. That can't be. You must be exaggerating." I'm not. And why should anything over 130 pounds feel like a weight that, for a woman, simply can't be right? Can't be healthy and totally beautiful and okay? Remember, I am still stocky and muscular. *That is my build. That will never change.* I'm always going to weigh more than many women my height and size, because I have more muscle mass. While it took me a long time to realize it, I now know my body will never look or feel good at anything near 130 pounds. It's just not the right number for me, the only person in the world who can be me.

And I am still surprised to see sometimes, on days when I have eaten lighter and the number on the scale goes up; *"149? Really?"* Then the next day, when I have indulged an awesome steak dinner, followed by dessert (because you need to do that sometimes) the number will then go down; *"143? Seriously, after that dinner? Heck yeah!"* This is because there are a thousand things going on in your miraculous body. It takes time for all the nutrients, protein, sodium, all of that food-science stuff to be processed, distributed where it's needed, and converted into muscle or energy, and the rest bypassed. The number on the scale may very well reflect your body's response to what you ate and did two days ago. If you realize this, you won't react so violently to an upswing, or a downswing. It should be used to monitor maintenance within a range that is healthy for you. A stop on the scale once a day is more than enough. I obviously wasn't capable of such restraint in the beginning and I was surprised to find my weight can sometimes increase or decrease as much as six pounds either way in one day. Just one day! A normal, Callie-is-healthy day. Whether I'm 143 or 149 at a given time on a given day matters none. Only that I am in my healthy range.

# About the Author

Callie is bold.  She is also healed and inspired to help others kick the shit out of this disease, just as she did.  She is you and she is also me.  Callie is the name I published under as she was brave and bold enough to tell this story, to put it out there to reach and impact others.  While I was not ready to become—to the rest of my professional and public world—the new face of bulimia, Callie was.  And I will be forever grateful.  She truly feels like a person of my past.  Someone I abused and tormented for years, but she, being me, is also strong and resilient and has forgiven me.

I hope her story will empower you.  If so, please share it.  And please let Callie know.


callie.bowld@gmail.com

Made in the USA
Coppell, TX
20 June 2020